Pat

111 Extreme Places
in Europe
That You
Shouldn't Miss

111

emons:

111 Extreme Places in Europe That You Shouldn't Miss is the book that accompanies the award-winning *Europe to the Maxx* series from Deutsche Welle's lifestyle and culture magazine "Euromaxx". Europe at its most extreme: this series makes Europe's architectural, natural, geographical and cultural superlatives experienceable by way of stunning high-quality travel reports. Watch around the world as part of the programme "Euromaxx", online at dw.com/lifestyle.

The book is a collaboration between Deutsche Welle (DW) and Emons Verlag.

© Emons Verlag GmbH
All rights reserved
Deutsche Welle (DW), Voltastraße 6, 13355 Berlin/Germany
Concept development and editing at Deutsche Welle:
Samira Schellhaaß, Patricia Szilagyi, Mirja Viehweger, Hendrik Welling
© Photographs, see page 238
© Cover icon: shutterstock.com / tassel78
Layout: Eva Kraskes, based on a design
by Lübbeke | Naumann | Thoben
Maps: altancicek.design, www.altancicek.de
Basic cartographical information from Openstreetmap,
© OpenStreetMap-Mitwirkende, OdbL
Editing: Martin Sketchley
Translation: Tom Ashforth
Printing and binding: Grafisches Centrum Cuno, Calbe
Printed in Germany 2021
ISBN 978-3-7408-1031-3
First edition

Did you enjoy this guidebook? Would you like to see more?
Join us in uncovering new places around the world on:
www.111places.com

Foreword

Being able to travel is a wonderful thing. I always bring new knowledge back with me from every journey. Yet there are some trips that stay with me more than others. This is when I have experienced something special, seen something unique or discovered something unprecedented. This book is full of these kinds of trips: 111 stories about record-breaking places. Landing at Barra airport in Scotland, for example, is unique as you touch down on Europe's only runway made of sand. At the same time it is a travel guide for European places, which you won't find gathered together like this in any other guidebook.

This collaboration between Deutsche Welle and Emons Verlag was inspired by the *Europe to the Maxx* series, which is part of Deutsche Welle's lifestyle and culture magazine "Euromaxx". This multiple award-winning series of films enables viewers to experience the most spectacular places in Europe. The reports, which can be found on YouTube, are also part of the book. Just scan the QR codes alongside the stories.

Whether it is a trip to the highest railway station on Jungfraujoch in Switzerland or to the biggest cuckoo clock in the world in the Black Forest, every story is one of a kind. Did you know that there is a Buddhist region in Europe? This was new to me and Euromaxx reporter Hendrik Welling's trip to Kalmykia on the southeast edge of Europe inspired me to make new travel plans. On the other hand, when I saw the same reporter fighting through a snowstorm on Europe's biggest glacier in Iceland I was more than happy that I could follow what he experienced on YouTube from the comfort of my sofa and read more about the history of the glacier in this book. A Persian proverb that my mother hung on the wall of our living room is quite apt here: 'The best way to come home from a journey is in one piece.' I wish you exciting yet safe fun reading this book!

Samira Schellhaaß, Head of Department Life and Style, Deutsche Welle

111 Extreme Places

Some of the stories in the book include
a QR code. Scanning these with a smartphone
will take you straight to the corresponding
video from the *Europe to the Maxx* series.

1 Fonderia Marinelli
The oldest bell casting workshop

The sound of church bells is ubiquitous in Agnone. The village in the Italian region of Molise has only 5,200 residents, but no less than 16 churches. This should come as no surprise, as it is also home to the oldest bell casting workshop in Europe. Surrounded by mountain peaks and wild nature, it feels as though time has stood still in Agnone. Fonderia Marinelli's bells are still produced in precisely the same way as they were hundreds of years ago.

The Marinelli bell casting workshop has been around since 1339. The craft has been passed down from generation to generation: from the manufacture of the clay mould, to the 'recipe' for the perfect bronze mixture of copper and tin. All of the steps in the process are carried out by hand to this day. The Marinellis believe that only in this way does a bell obtain not only its unique sound, but also its soul. Their bells have borne the Pope's seal since 1924.

Every bell is unique, every form is specially fabricated. It takes at least three months, from the first drawings to the decisive last step, the casting – and that is very much like a religious ritual. There is often a priest present, who says prayers and blesses the bell. The bronze is heated to more than 1,100 °C, and flows into the mould like glowing lava. Whether the result is good can only be assessed a few days later when the metal has cooled. After the clay casing is peeled off and it has been polished, the 'Maestro Campanale' checks the sound of every bell. Only then is the instrument sent out into the world.

From the leaning tower of Pisa, to the UNO in New York and the Vatican, bells from Agnone can be heard in countless places around the world. And because the Marinellis hand down not only their knowledge but also their love of the craft from one generation to the next, there are sure to be a whole lot more to come – each and every one manufactured according to ancient tradition.

Address Via Felice D'Onofrio 14, 86081 Agnone, Italy | **Getting there** Agnone is around 220 kilometres from Rome. You can take the train to Isernia, and from there the bus to Agnone. | **Tip** In the Fonderia Marinelli museum you can see the largest collection of bronze bells in the world. The oldest bell exhibited is around 1,000 years old. Guided tours daily (www.campanemarinelli.com).

2__Alnwick Poison Garden

The most dangerous garden

England is the kingdom of gardeners. The passion of the British for anything that blossoms is unrivalled. A paradise of green meadows and colourful flowers also welcomes visitors to the garden of Alnwick Castle. The castle, located in the far north of England, has belonged to the family of the Duke of Northumberland for 700 years. The path through the castle garden leads between fragrant rose bushes and cherry trees blossoming in delicate pinks, until you suddenly find yourself in front of a wrought-iron gate with two skulls. This is the entrance to the most dangerous part of the property: Alnwick Poison Garden.

'These plants can kill' is written in large letters on the gate, and you are only allowed to enter in the company of a guide. The rules of conduct for visitors are strict: plants must not be touched or smelled. These precautions are absolutely justified – the most poisonous plants in the world are all gathered here. These include intoxicating plants such as cannabis or the opium poppy, but also seductively beautiful specimens such as angel trumpets or wolfsbane, which seem to disguise their toxic nature with their vibrant-coloured flowers.

The spectrum of potential effects ranges from slightly numbing to absolutely deadly. Hemlock, for example, was historically served as a drug to perform executions! The Greek philosopher Socrates famously chose a cup of hemlock to bring about his death. Wolfsbane, meanwhile, was used to contaminate the wells of the enemy, and castor beans, the oil of which is often found in medicines or in cosmetic products, contains one of the strongest natural poisons in existence.

Nevertheless, you shouldn't be worried about visiting Alnwick Poison Garden. Thanks to the knowledgeable guides, you should leave the Poison Garden not only fit and healthy, but educated in a wealth of floral poisons.

Address Denwick Lane, Alnwick NE66 1YU, England | **Getting there** Alnwick is nearer to Edinburgh than London – from the Scottish capital take the train to Alnmouth, then the bus to Alnwick (Playhouse). | **Hours** Daily 10am–6pm (shortened hours in the winter months) | **Tip** Alnwick Castle itself is also worth a visit: the historic walls served as Hogwarts School of Witchcraft and Wizardry in the Harry Potter films.

3 Alto Douro

The oldest wine-growing region

The Douro cuts deep into the landscape of north-east Portugal. Here, near the border with Spain, the river meanders through innumerable shale hills. Lush vineyards rise up to either side of the river's banks. The radiant white walls of the wine estates, the so-called *quintas*, flash through the green vines every now and then.

Wine has been grown in Alto Douro, the 'high Douro', for more than 2,000 years. The Romans recognised the ideal conditions of the dry-hot climate and planted vines here. Many centuries later, in 1756, the borders of the region were officially defined for the first time. With this, the Alto Douro became the first legally pro-tected wine-growing region in the world. It even became a UNESCO World Heritage Site in 2001.

The region remains one of the most important wine regions in Europe to this day. Vintners cultivate grapes here on around 25,000 hectares of land. History and tradition are particularly impor-tant to them. The grapes are still picked by hand, as the slopes are too steep for machines, and the mash is still trampled by foot at most of the vineyards, just as it always has been.

This is also how one of the most famous wines in the world is made: port. The Alto Douro region is the cradle of this sophisti-cated drink, and the sweet fortified wine can only be pressed out of the grapes that grow here. After the pressing, the grape must is mixed with high-proof brandy. This stops the fermentation, and provides for port's characteristic taste as well as a high alcohol con-tent of around 20 per cent by volume. The famous beverage obtains its final aroma near the city that also gave it its name: Porto. It matures for at least two years in one of the many wineries around the harbour city. Only then is it exported to a myriad of countries, taking the taste of the oldest wine-growing region in Europe out into the whole world.

Getting there From Porto you can reach the region of Alto Douro by car, train or boat. Particularly recommended is the 'Linha do Douro'. The train journey leads from Porto to Pocinho along the Douro, and is one of the prettiest train routes in Europe. | Tip Many of the traditional *quintas* along the Douro provide tours that include wine tasting.

The QR code takes you to the corresponding video in the series, *Europe to the Maxx*. Look for more QR codes placed on the photos in 19 other chapters.

4 Trollveggen
The highest rock face

Åndalsnes, around 400 kilometres north-west of Oslo, is the climbing capital of Norway. With around 2,200 inhabitants, the town is located in the middle of the Romsdal Alps. While it is actually more of a village, in summer it can get quite busy, as this is when hikers and climbers from all over the world visit Åndalsnes. They are attracted by the easy access to fjords, mountain streams and imposing rock formations right on their doorstep.

The best-known of these is only a few kilometres away: it is called Trollveggen – in English 'Troll Wall'. The distinctive rock face is part of the Trolltindene massif, which provides a spectacular backdrop to Åndalsnes. The Troll Wall towers around 1,700 metres above the valley, with a series of characteristic jagged rocks on the summit. According to legend, they are petrified trolls – a deep-rooted part of local mythology.

It is not the height alone that makes the Troll Wall stand out, however: what fascinates most climbers is the steep face, which soars up vertically for around one kilometre. In parts, the rock face even has an overhang of up to 50 metres – an extreme challenge even for professional climbers. For a long time the Troll Wall was therefore considered unassailable. Nevertheless, the most courageous climbers tried, and a competition began regarding who would be the first to complete the climb. This was finally achieved in 1965, when two expeditions conquered the vertical rock face at the same time. They took 14 days to struggle to the summit via two different routes.

Today, there are a dozen or so climbing routes, but none of them are suitable for amateurs. However, there is still a lot to experience for those who do not want to explore the rock wall with such intimacy. The area offers numerous hiking routes for all levels of fitness and ability, often with spectacular views of the famous Troll Wall.

Address 6300 Åndalsnes, Norway | Getting there By train or bus from Oslo to Åndalsnes, where numerous operators offer tours to the Troll Wall | Tip Take a trip along the nearby Trollstigen road, which winds through the Trolltindene massif in 11 hairpin bends, and offers impressive views.

5___Andorra la Vella

The highest capital

Very few people would use the word 'pretty' to describe the capital of
Andorra. Shopping streets and shopping malls dominate the image
of this city, which is home to 23,000 people. Andorra is not part of
the EU, and is seen as a tax haven. As a result, many tourists visit
for the sole purpose of engaging in some cheap retail therapy. While
Andorra la Vella has attuned itself to shoppers' needs, this means
that day trippers often miss out on the city's most important sights,
related to its exposed location: the fabulous mountain landscape of
the surrounding area.

Andorra la Vella is located in a high valley in the eastern Pyrenees, at an altitude of more than 1,000 metres. Just beyond the
edges of the city, the mountains rise up and nature takes over. It
is a paradise for fans of the outdoors and extreme sports. Mountain bike tours, canyoning trips and climbing tours – availability of
such a diversity of activities around a capital is very rare. There are
65 peaks over 2,000 metres to discover in the most condensed of
spaces, as the small principality is one of Europe's mini states. It's
possible to drive from the border with France in the north-east to
the Spanish border in the south in less than one hour – despite the
fact that it's not possible to drive particularly fast due to the winding mountain roads.

In summer, alongside adventure holidaymakers, lots of hikers and
anglers are drawn to the Pyrenees, while in winter it's the skiers who
visit. They all experience the purest of nature very near to the city.
Indeed, 90 per cent of Andorra is undeveloped. The sharp peaks and
narrow valleys seem to resist civilisation. Only here and there does
the occasional village church tower rise in the landscape. Andorra is
like an island in the middle of Europe, with a capital whose location is its biggest trump card: the unique proximity to nature and
the mountains.

Address Andorra la Vella, AD 500, Andorra | Getting there Andorra doesn't have its own airport, but you can fly to Barcelona or Toulouse, then travel by bus or rental car. | Tip When you visit Andorra you should try *Nectum*, a pine cone syrup, that's said to have magical powers.

6 __ Llanfairpwllgwyn-gyllgogerychwyrndro-bwllllantysiliogogogoch

The town with the longest name

The island of Anglesey off the north-west coast of Wales is a peaceful place. Very few tourists stray this far out, as there are hardly any attractions. It does have a significant history, however. Anglesey – or Ynys Môn, as it is called in Welsh – was a centre of the druid culture, and for many centuries served as a place of refuge for the Celtic high priests. Numerous myths surrounding this period live on to this day.

One place especially feels like a relict from this era. Llanfair-pwllgwyngyllgogerychwyrndrobwllllantysiliogogogoch is the name of the 3,000-resident village in the south-east of the island. This translates in English as: The church of Mary in the hollow of the white hazel near the fierce whirlpool and the church of Tysilio by the red cave. With 58 letters, it's the longest single-word place name anywhere in Europe. Pronouncing it correctly is an almost impossible task for non-Welsh speakers, and even those who live on the island simply call the village 'Llanfairpwll' for the sake of convenience.

But if you suspected this might be a legacy of the Celts, you're wrong. The almost unpronounceable name is in fact a very recent invention. The village was connected to the railway network in the middle of the 19th century. Craftspeople and traders settled here, but business was slow. An ingenious cobbler invented the tongue twister in order to make the place more interesting. His creative strategy worked, the Welsh village became well-known around the United Kingdom, and attracted an increasing number of visitors.

Today people are still drawn to the village due to its unusual name, with the sign at the railway station popular for photos by tourists. And with its tongue twister, Llanfairpwll even secured an entry in the *Guinness Book of Records*.

Address LL61 5UJ, Anglesey, Wales | Getting there From Liverpool or Manchester you can reach Llanfairpwll in around 3.5 hours by train. | Tip Plas Newydd, a manor house from the late Middle Ages near Llanfairpwll, is worth a visit. The property is open to visitors and home to several exhibitions.

7 — Fuggerei
The oldest social housing complex

The gates of the Fuggerei close at 10pm precisely. Those who want to be let in after this time have to make a small payment to the night watchman. That is not the only thing that still works as it did around 500 years ago, here in the oldest social housing complex in Europe.

Jakob Fugger donated the housing complex to his Bavarian home town in 1521. The businessman, trader and banker was considered the richest man in the world at the time. He didn't just want his wealth to multiply, however: he also wanted to use it to help the needy. So with the Fuggerei, just a few minutes' walk from the centre of Augsburg, a small city within the city was created. Surrounded by an outer wall, 67 uniform houses line up in eight terraces. The apartments were modern and fully furnished, even with their own bathrooms – a real luxury for the time.

Around 150 people live here today, all of them, as was the case at the time of the Fuggerei's establishment, destitute Augsburg citizens. This is how the charitable donor decreed it. The basic rent remains the equivalent of a Rheinish guilder. What was then around a week's wages for a day labourer, is today just 88 cents – per year! This makes the roughly 60-square-metre apartments of the Fuggerei the cheapest rental apartments in Europe. The housing complex is financed by endowments and the admission of visiting tourists.

However, the residents must meet one condition: they should say three prayers a day for the donor and his family. Jakob Fugger was a devout Catholic, and there is much to suggest that he didn't only have benefaction in mind when building the housing complex, but also wanted to secure God's favour for himself and his family. However, that surely doesn't matter to either the residents of the Fuggerei, or its visitors, who get a rare insight into social housing and life around 500 years ago.

Address Jakoberstraße 26, 86152 Augsburg, Germany | Getting there From Augsburg main station you can walk to the Fuggerei in about 20 minutes, or take tram line 23. | Hours Apr–Sept daily 9am–8pm, Oct–Mar 9am–6pm, closed Christmas Eve | Tip If you'd like to get an insight into how the residents of the Fuggerei live today, view the display apartment at Ochsengasse 51.

8__ Camp Nou
The largest stadium

For fans of the FC Barcelona football team, this is almost a holy site: Camp Nou, the 'new pitch', which was called Estadi del Futbol Club Barcelona until 2001. It is the home ground of *their* team, and responsible for the emergence of a whole series of world-famous footballers: Lionel Messi, Andrés Iniesta, Xavi, Gerard Piqué, Pep Guardiola – they all became big names here.

It is no surprise, then, that even on days when there is no game, a long queue is already forming in front of the main entrance to the stadium in the early morning. Alongside Sagrada Família, Parc Güell and the Picasso Museum, Camp Nou is part of every sightseeing tour in Barcelona.

It is not just an ordinary stadium, no simple football ground – it is more of a pilgrimage site for football fans from all over the world. And they get to see quite a lot on a tour through the biggest stadium in Europe. There is space for almost 100,000 people on the Camp Nou terraces, and after a planned conversion there should even be room for a few thousand more.

Inside the stadium is also the FC Barcelona museum. Here visitors can marvel at the club's various trophies, and succumb completely to the cult of Messi and co. You also get to see the commentators' boxes, the away team's changing room, and the coach's bench from close proximity on a guided tour. Finally, visitors can – at least almost – feel like a real football star themselves, when they walk through the players' tunnel and enter the stadium.

That the cult of football in Camp Nou has long since taken on an other-worldly character is demonstrated not least by FC Barcelona's plans for an urn hall in the stadium. In future, around 30,000 fans could find their final resting place here, and thus show their loyalty to the club even after their passing. That is the only logical next step for the temple of football that is Camp Nou.

Address C. Arístides Maillol 12, 08028 Barcelona, Spain | **Getting there** From Barcelona city centre by metro (line 3 to Collblanc, or line 5 to Les Corts); buses and trams also stop nearby | **Hours** Guided tours daily apart from on match days, Dec 25 and Jan 1; the museum is also open on match days | **Tip** Only a few metres from Camp Nou is La Masia, FC Barcelona's youth academy. Messi, Xavi and Iniesta among many others began their careers in this pretty, historic building.

9 __ Barra Airport
The only airport on a beach

Baggage chaos, long queues at check-in, and endless security procedures: travellers struggle with these problems at most of the world's airports these days. This is not the case in Barra, however. Things are a whole lot more sedate at this small Scottish island's airport, as the staff here only have around 8,000 passengers a year to process. The pilots, on the other hand, face a very specific challenge when flying into Barra, as the airport is on the beach; or more precisely, the beach *is* the airport.

When the tide is in, the three runways are completely flooded with water from the North Atlantic. As a result the time frame for flight operations is dictated by nature, as aircraft can only take off or land when the tide is out. At this time the windsocks are raised, which indicates that the beach is closed to walkers.

A scheduled flight from Glasgow visits the island, which belongs to the Outer Hebrides, two or three times a day. Due to the special conditions, only small planes are in operation on the route. The landing approach is not easy: there are no signal lights or colour markings, with only a couple of posts in the sand for guidance. There is also usually a strong wind to contend with. Landings can therefore take several attempts before they are successful. And if the landing is not achieved in time, then aircraft can be forced to return to their point of origin.

The unusual airport experiences around 1,400 take-offs and landings a year. Most passengers are locals, but Barra is also attracting an increasing number of tourists and plane-spotters. As soon as the tide goes out, they start waiting for the perfect shot: that moment when a small aircraft touches down on the wet sand. And even many experienced pilots want to land an aircraft at Barra at least once in their career. Where else do they get to take a stroll on the beach right after touchdown?

Address Eoligarry, Barra HS9 5YD, Scotland | Getting there Barra Airport is only served by Glasgow, although the outward journey is also possible by ferry from Oban on the Scottish mainland. | Tip Kisimul Castle in the south of the island is worth a visit. This 15th-century castle is situated on a rocky island in the sea, and can only be reached by boat.

10 Aire de Berchem
The biggest petrol station

A pharmacist was the first petrol station attendant in the world. Bertha Benz bought all of the petrol supplies from a pharmacy in the small city of Wiesloch in Baden-Württemberg in 1888. The automotive pioneer was en route from Mannheim to Pforzheim and needed to refuel on the long journey. This was the first overland tour in history, and petrol stations had not yet been introduced.

Nowadays it's impossible to imagine our roads and motorways without them, with petrol stations on all large road junctions, motorways and main roads. While they are generally functional, nondescript buildings, some stand out. One such example is Aire de Berchem, the biggest petrol station in Europe.

The Luxembourgish village of Berchem doesn't even have 900 residents, but the petrol tourists, who visit every day, surpass this number many times over. Around 7,500 cars and 1,500 lorries roll in daily. On an area the size of eight football pitches are 51 pumps – and it isn't rare for them all to be in use at the same time. It requires 20 to 30 tankers a day to keep the tanks at this gigantic station replenished. Meanwhile, tourists and hobby photographers visit Berchem just to watch the goings on. The petrol station as a tourist attraction – the pharmacist from Wiesloch surely couldn't have imagined such a scenario.

The reason for the popularity of this petrol station is simple: the low price of the fuel. There is nowhere else in Western Europe where you can refuel your vehicle as cheaply as in Luxembourg. This is made possible by the grand duchy's low petroleum tax. And as neighbouring countries are not far away, drivers from Belgium, France, the Netherlands and Germany travel to Aire de Berchem to refuel. This could of course change should alternative forms of propulsion ever catch on, but for the moment, Berchem will remain the fuel capital of Europe.

Address 3321 Berchem, Luxembourg | Getting there Aire de Berchem is on the A 3/E 25 between Croix de Gasperich and Livange and can be reached by car in around half an hour from Luxembourg City. | Hours Daily 9am–midnight | Tip If you need to recover from all that driving, why not visit the nearby Parc Merveilleux, the only zoo in Luxembourg? Alongside the animals, there are also adventure playgrounds and a large forest area.

11__Zoological Garden
The most species-rich zoo

More than 28,000 animals from over 1,300 species: this diversity is what makes the Zoological Garden in former West Berlin unique. From aardvarks and antelopes via giraffes and gorillas to zebras. A single visit really isn't enough to see every species in this zoo.

Berlin's Zoological Garden had very small beginnings, however, with only 47 animals at its opening in 1844, having been entrusted to its operators by King Frederick William IV of Prussia. Over time the Zoological Garden became a popular leisure attraction for Berliners and visitors alike, and grew vigorously, with more and more exotic species added.

But it is not only the sheer volume of animals that attracts around five million visitors a year: it is the individual zoo residents, which have been given affectionate names such as Bulette (meatball), Knorke (great) or Knautschke (crumply). Animal contemporaries who won the hearts of Berliners, whose pain and pleasure they shared, and whose losses they grieved like the death of a relative. They are the secret of the zoo's success.

Bobby the gorilla was the first to make the step up to visitors' favourite in 1928. The little ape came from Marseille to Berlin in style, travelling with his keeper in a first-class rail compartment. After his early death he was immortalised in granite, and adorns the zoo's logo to this day. Later on hippopotamus Knautschke also achieved similar prominence. The animal survived not only the bombings of World War II, but, thanks to food donations from the city's inhabitants, also the Berlin blockade. Then there's the polar bear baby Knut. Shunned by his mother, the white ball of fur was selflessly reared by his keeper. Most recently, the long-awaited panda offspring secured a place in the hearts of the zoo's visitors. It is the small and large animal stars that make the Zoological Garden in the German capital so special.

Address Hardenbergplatz 8, 10787 Berlin, Germany | **Getting there** From Berlin main station by S-Bahn, U-Bahn or bus to Zoologischer Garten | **Hours** Daily 9am–6.30pm, shorter hours in winter | **Tip** The site covers 33 hectares. If you are exploring the zoo with children or have lots of baggage with you, rent a handcart at the Löwentor.

12 Jungfraujoch
The highest railway station

In August 1893, Swiss industrialist Adolf Guyer-Zeller made a bold decision: he wanted to build a railway that would lead up to the peak of the 4,158-metre Jungfrau. Up until that time, ascending the third-highest mountain in the Bernese Alps, with its eternal blanket of snow, was reserved for experienced mountaineers only. The first successful climb to the summit did not take place until 1811, and the planned railway line was intended to make it more widely accessible.

It took 16 years from the breaking of ground to the completion of the route. The line doesn't go all the way up to the summit as Guyer-Zeller had envisaged, but with its terminus on the Jungfraujoch at 3,454 metres, its construction at this altitude is still considered an engineering masterstroke. If that wasn't enough, more than half of the nine-kilometre track is in a tunnel, which had to be cut by hand. On 1 August, 1912, the Swiss national holiday, the first train finally made the whole journey from the mountain pass Kleine Scheidegg up to the Jungfraujoch.

The trip takes around half an hour, during which time the cogwheel train ascends an elevation of around 1,400 metres. In order to better acclimatise visitors to the mountain air, there is an intermediate stop at the Eismeer station. From here visitors already have a clear view of the famous triumvirate Eiger, Mönch and Jungfrau.

The terminus of the railway is in a tunnel, but when you step out on to the viewing platform, it's likely that you'll have your breath taken away – and not only because of the thin air. When the weather's good, a unique mountain panorama with around 200 alpine peaks opens up, with the snow-covered summits of Jungfrau and Mönch seemingly close enough to touch. That's when the fascination that may have moved Guyer-Zeller to make his daring plan a reality more than 125 years ago really becomes apparent.

Address Jungfraujoch, 3984 Fieschertal, Switzerland | **Getting there** By train from Bern via Interlaken and Lauterbrunnen to Kleine Scheidegg. The Jungfraubahn travels from here up to Jungfraujoch. | **Hours** The train rides daily from 8am up to Jungfraujoch. The last return trip varies according to the season. | **Tip** One of the attractions on the Jungfraujoch is the ice palace. Marvel at countless ice sculptures in the grotto, which covers around 1,000 square metres.

13__Velocity 2
The fastest zip line

'Three, two one!' calls a member of staff – and then you're off! Slowly at first, then rapidly accelerating. Tied up like a Christmas present, riders hang horizontally in the air and race along the steel line towards the abyss. Only a couple of carabiners stand between adrenalin junkies and a fall to the depths, which would almost certainly be fatal.

Thrill-seekers whoosh over the moon-like landscape of the former slate quarry, sometimes only a few metres above the craggy rocks, at speeds up to 160 kilometres an hour! The brilliant blue lake of Llyn Dinas is certainly a highlight for anyone who still manages to enjoy the view, with riders zooming over the water on the zip line as if they're flying. The ride is around one-and-a-half-kilometres long, a distance which is covered in less than a minute.

This zip line is the fastest adventure of its kind in Europe. Those who want to experience the unique rush it provides will have to travel to the north of Wales. Snowdonia National Park is located in a region full of impressive mountain ranges, with the name derived from the country's highest mountain: Mount Snowdon.

This area was once dominated by mining, but as this industry has waned its place has been taken by adventure tourism. Several outdoor companies have established themselves in the area, offering a wide range of activities with the potential for thrills, with everything from zip lines to surfing on artificial waves and jumping on underground trampolines.

Where generations of men once toiled away underground, recreational fun is now the order of the day. Wales wants to establish itself as Britain's centre of adventure, very much based on the model of New Zealand, the home of many extreme sports. With impressive attractions like the fastest zip line in Europe, the country is racing towards this goal at breakneck speed.

Address Zip World, Penrhyn Quarry, Bethesda, LL57 4YG, Gwynedd, Wales | **Getting there** Around 1.5 hours by car from Manchester or Liverpool | **Hours** Daily apart from Dec 25 and 26 | **Tip** Those who would rather experience the landscape of the national park in the old-fashioned way should hike the 1,085-metre Mount Snowdon – just consider the weather carefully first. Sir Edmund Hillary trained for the ascent of Mount Everest here.

14 Eden Project
The largest indoor rainforest

Whether the Biblical Garden of Eden ever actually existed is uncertain, but it was supposed to have been a green paradise, a place in which humans lived in harmony with nature. Today this vision seems to have become a reality in the south of England, and can be found in the county of Cornwall: the present day Garden of Eden.

It took six years to bring the Eden Project to life, to turn a wasteland where clay was mined in the past, into a fertile oasis. The Eden Project covers an area of 50 hectares, and features around 100,000 plants from all around the world. In this way, reproductions of biotopes from different climate zones of the Earth were created – the natural landscapes of the world in small format.

Two greenhouses in the form of geodesic domes cover part of the site, looking like large soap bubbles that have stuck to one another. Inside these domes stable climatic conditions are maintained, and the lush vegetation unfurls under the honeycombed hexagons of plastic foil. The free-standing structures are up to 50 metres high and 240 metres wide, gigantic constructions that nonetheless seem surprisingly delicate.

The larger of the two greenhouses is home to the largest covered rainforest in the world. Mangroves, rubber trees, ferns, banana plants and palms grow here, in tropical temperatures on a 16,000-square-metre area of land. The result is a thick, jungle-like environment that visitors can explore.

Those who wish to do so can learn everything about this precious biotope here. The Eden Project is, after all, not an amusement park, but is an educational centre and environmental organisation. The core idea is that only those who experience the beauty of nature and engage with it can also protect it – an issue that seems more urgent today than ever. Otherwise, humankind is threatened with no less than the definitive banishment from paradise.

Address Bodelva, PL24 2SG, Cornwall, England | **Getting there** From London by train to St Austell, from there by 101 bus. Visitors arriving by public transport, bicycle or on foot pay reduced admission. | **Hours** All year, current information at www.edenproject.com | **Tip** Every summer concerts take place featuring renowned musicians from around the world, during which the Eden Project's greenhouse domes are illuminated atmospherically.

15 __ Nausicaá
The biggest aquarium

The sea has traditionally played the main role in Boulogne-sur-Mer, as the city around 30 kilometres south of Calais is home to the largest fishing harbour in France. And not far from the fishing boats, right on the water, is the Nausicaá sea centre – a gigantic monument to the underwater world.

The modern building already pays homage to one of the most impressive sea dwellers, the manta ray, on the outside, while inside visitors can admire these up to eight-metre giants in the flesh. It is one of the 1,600 species that can be marvelled at in the numerous aquariums of Nausicaá, as winding corridors lead the visitor through a subaquatic world, which for many of them is simultaneously eerie and fascinating.

One of the attraction's greatest features is its compact nature: in one tank colourful tropical fish frolic among coral reefs, while in the next delicate shimmering jellyfish float weightlessly in their liquid environment. A few metres further on visitors can watch how sea lions – cumbersome and awkward when on land – are able to glide elegantly through the water. And in an 18-metre glass tunnel it's possible to be surrounded by sharks, rays and large shoals of fish, and feel immersed in the underwater world.

A special highlight awaits towards the end of the circuit: the biggest aquarium tank in Europe. An ecosystem is reconstructed in 10 million litres of water that mimics what might be found off a Colombian island thousands of kilometres away. Visitors can experience the world of the Pacific Ocean through the 100-square-metre pane of glass, as goliath groupers, schools of sardines and even hammerhead sharks pass right before their eyes. Then, finally, the giant manta rays. Even experienced divers only rarely get a glimpse of these impressive creatures, but a visit to Nausicaá allows even non-swimmers to explore the wonders of the seven seas.

Address Boulevard Sainte-Beuve, 62203 Boulogne-sur-Mer, France | **Getting there** You can reach the aquatic centre in around 2.5 hours by car from Paris, alternatively by train from Paris via Calais, onwards by bus (line F). | **Hours** Daily 9.30am – 6.30pm, closed 25 Dec and 6 – 24 Jan | **Tip** The nearby museum Maison de la Beurière shows how fishermen lived towards the end of the 19th century.

16__Delirium Café

The bar with the largest selection of beer

Germany is considered a country of beer drinkers, but Belgium is the country of beer variety. It's therefore hardly surprising that a bar has capitalised on precisely this fact. The Delirium Café in Brussels has even made it into the *Guinness Book of Records*, with 2,004 types of beer on the menu. That was around 15 years ago, since which time other beers have been added – but who can keep up with so many to choose from?

The bar found its home in a vaulted cellar from the 18th century in the middle of Brussels old town. Beer mugs and serving trays with the logos of beer brands from all around the world hang from the ceiling. Innumerable bottles with colourful labels stand on shelves ready to be ordered. The drinks menu is 192 pages long, but don't worry – the barkeeper will be happy to advise anyone who is struggling to choose.

There are many types of beer from Belgium to try, but also offerings from more distant countries: from Indonesia to China, Mexico to Peru, from Korea to the Congo. Classic styles are on offer, such as Pils, ales or stouts, but also fruit beers or those with unusual ingredients such as chocolate or chilli. Most are from small breweries, like the house beer 'Delirium Tremens', which gave the bar its name. This strong pale blond, which tastes of herbs, spices and dried fruits and is produced in a private brewery in east Flanders, is the most popular beer on the menu. The most expensive is '3 Fonteinen Hommage', a fruit lambic with raspberries and sour cherries, which costs €110 a bottle. Whether it's worth the rather steep price is up to you to decide!

Should you ever grow tired of beer, you could always switch to one of the other bars located in the 'Delirium Village' that has grown up around the pub. Their menus are dominated by absinths, rums or tequilas, with several hundreds of varieties available at any one time.

Address Impasse de la Fidélité 4, 1000 Brussels, Belgium | **Getting there** Delirium Café is a five-minute walk from Brussels' main station. | **Hours** Mon–Thu 6pm–4am, Fri & Sat 10–6am, Sun 10–3am | **Tip** It is especially worth visiting on Thursdays, when there are live music and jam sessions.

17 Palace of the Parliament
The building with the largest floor area

It is the stone memorial of a dark chapter in the country's history. You can see it from far away: Bucharest's Palace of the Parliament, which towers up, monumental and monstrous, in the middle of the Romanian capital. It bears witness to the megalomania of a power-hungry dictator.

Nicolae Ceaușescu had the 'People's House', as it was called back then, built in gigantic dimensions in 1984, as a symbol of his power. A three-kilometre-long boulevard was to lead up to this ostentatious building. The sacrifices the general population were forced to make were considerable. For the palace and boulevard, the dictator had part of the old town, including churches and synagogues, torn down, and more than 50,000 families were forcibly resettled to make way for the grand project. A large part of the state's funds were pumped into the building. 20,000 labourers as well as 400 architects and engineers were employed around the clock in three shifts in order to make Ceaușescu's dream a reality. Food and electricity were rationed for Romanians. The people starved, while the dictator built.

A building of superlatives was created under these conditions. The largest hall in the palace measures 2,200 square metres, with a total of 365,000 square metres spread over 12 floors. Many of the 5,300 rooms, halls and corridors are adorned with crystal chandeliers and marble columns. 31 lifts and 2,000 kilometres of electric wiring were installed.

But political change came before the palace could be completed. Revolutions in the Eastern Bloc also led to the collapse of the socialist system in Romania and the overthrow of Ceaușescu, but his hugely over-sized pompous building remained standing. Today the building is the seat of the Chamber of Deputies and the Senate, and has become one of the city's biggest tourist attractions, as an unmissable historical monument.

Address Strada Izvor 2–4, Bucharest, Romania | Getting there From the main station in Bucharest Gara de Nord with metro 1 or bus 123 to Pod Izvor, from there take line 136 to Casa Academiei | Hours Viewing 9am–4pm, book in advance on +40 (0)733 558102 or cic.vizite@cdep.ro | Tip The national museum is housed on the other side of the building. Alongside a large collection of Romanian art, there are many international works on show.

18_ Budapest

The biggest spa city

Thick clouds of steam hang above the tender yellow, palace-like building of the Széchenyi baths. Budapest's most popular thermal bath is full – and it is like this every season. Tourists and locals alike populate the 15 pools of the bath house. Swimmers do their lengths in cooler water at a temperature of 26 °C, while a couple of older gentlemen have made themselves comfortable with their chess board in the neighbouring pool at a pleasant 38 °C. For many locals, a visit to one of the city's dozen thermal baths is simply part of everyday life. People meet, discuss the latest news, talk about work or seal deals.

That there are so many spas in the Hungarian capital is due to the huge subterranean lake that lies below the Carpathian Basin. Some 1,000 metres below the ground, the water heats up due to its proximity to the Earth's core. And because a fissure runs through the stone stratum right underneath Budapest, this water forces its way to the surface with temperatures of up to 76 °C, enriched with minerals that are purported to have curative effects. There are 123 such natural springs around the city. The Romans were the first to make use of them when they settled in the region around 2,000 years ago. Back then, the climate was not so mild, and the soldiers were cold, so they redirected the warm water that bubbled up from the ground into warming baths. They called their city Aquincum: 'lots of water'. 1,500 years later the Ottomans also built spas here – similar to the hammams in their homelands.

The Hungarians continued these traditions after many wars and revolutions. Baths such as Széchenyi in the district of Pest, Gellért bath on the Buda side or Rudas bath, which dates back to the time of the Ottomans, are well known even beyond the country's borders. They continuously attract visitors from all around the world to Europe's biggest spa city.

Getting there Budapest is well connected through its airport and three large railway stations, while within the city you should travel by metro where possible. | Tip Right next to the Lukács bath is the entrance to the Molnár-János cave, where experienced divers can make cave expeditions in warm thermal water.

19 __ Athos

The only region that only men can enter

It is the entry ticket to a very unique world: without a Diamonitirion, a kind of visa, it is not possible to enter the monks' republic of Athos. Only 100 orthodox pilgrims a day are issued such a permit, along with another 10 non-orthodox visitors. Access is strictly controlled, and it is necessary for every visitor to fulfil a single requirement: they have to be a man.

The outermost headland of the Chalkidiki peninsula belongs to Greece, but is also autonomous. Orthodox monks have lived around holy Mount Athos for more than 1,000 years, and there are 20 large monasteries and numerous smaller communities located here. The monks live according to centuries-old rules, with their daily life defined by prayer and church services. Some have even secluded themselves as hermits in remote caves. Faith, humbleness and chastity are the most important rules. These also include the so-called 'Ávaton', the ban on access for women – something that applies even to female animals. This is because for orthodox monks, Athos is considered the garden of Mother Mary – and is therefore reserved solely and exclusively for her presence. Fences, walls and barbed wire protect the men's world from unwanted female intruders, and even the tourist and fishing boats have to maintain a distance of least 500 metres from the shore.

The male pilgrims who are allowed to visit Athos benefit from a detailed insight into the everyday life of the monks, for whom manual tasks and self-sufficiency are just as much a part of their existence as prayer. The pilgrims are allowed to stay for four days, being accommodated each night in a different monastery. Of course, they must subordinate themselves completely to the customs of the monks. This starts with the greeting: whenever they encounter one of the monks, according to old tradition, they show their respect by saying 'Evlogite!' – 'bless me!'.

Address Athos, Chalkidiki, Greece | **Getting there** From Thessaloniki by bus to border town Ouranoupoli. Here you receive the Diamonitirion, for which you should apply around two months in advance. Then travel by boat to Daphni, the port of entry to Athos. | **Tip** On a trip on the tourist steamer, everyone – including women – can see the monasteries and the holy mountain from a distance. The trip along the south coast of the peninsula takes three to four hours, starting at Ouranoupoli.

20__Mondial Air Ballons
The biggest hot-air balloon meeting

Once a year things get very colourful above Chambley-Bussières. Every summer, up to 500 hot-air balloons at a time populate the sky above the Lorraine region near Metz, as pilots from around 40 nations participate in the Mondial Air Ballons festival in north-eastern France. For a 10-day period they guarantee a unique spectacle at lofty heights, with regular mass take offs from the three-kilometre runway of the former military airport.

The hot-air balloon meet has taken place since 1989, and is the biggest of its kind in Europe. That it is being held in France is no coincidence, as this country is the birthplace of modern balloon travel. The Montgolfier brothers flew the first large balloon in the court of King Louis XVI in 1783. A sheep, a cockerel and a duck were apparently the passengers on this first, historic trip, which saw the balloon in the air for eight minutes. A short time later, Frenchman Jean-François Pilâtre de Rozier was the first human passenger, reaching a height of around 26 metres by hot-air balloon. It was one of his descendants, Philippe Buron Pilâtre, who initiated the festival in Chambley.

The maxim for the Mondial festival is 'get up early!' as instruction for the first start begins at 6am. Permission to lift-off is only granted if weather conditions are good – that is, no rain, and not too much wind. Balloon piloting is an activity in which not everything can be calculated in advance, with every trip presenting different challenges. For example, while pilots know where the lift-off site is, it's very difficult for them to predict where they will land! It is that uncertainty that appeals to many festival participants, as they look forward to the excitement each take off brings. And so they return to the festival every year to float over the cornfields and meadows of Lorraine, offering a unique picture in the sky above France for spectators on the ground.

Address Aérodrome de Chambley, 11 Boulevard Antoine de Saint-Exupéry, 54470 Hagéville, France | **Getting there** Train to Metz, from there around 35 kilometres by rental car | **Tip** A special highlight during the festival is 'night glowing': the balloons remain on the ground, but are brightly lit by their burners.

21 Vai Beach

The largest natural palm grove

They suddenly appear like a Fata Morgana: the palm trees of Vai. Initially they are few and far between, but then there are more and more of them. To get here you'll have driven for kilometres on the eastern side of Crete, through dusty hills and barren plains, with no sign of trees for a considerable distance – only the occasional low-growing bush, serving as food for the free-roaming goats. But then, just before you reach the coast of the largest Greek island, a green oasis unexpectedly unfolds, with the forest of palms.

The road leads through the palm grove down to the beach. In a bay, the view opens out on to the turquoise sea. Small islands of rock jut out of the clear water, while in the foreground is a beach of light-coloured sand and gravel, lined with palm trees, giving a sense of the Pacific in the middle of Europe. More than 5,000 date palms transform the Mediterranean landscape into a Caribbean dream. It is the largest naturally growing palm grove in Europe. No surprise, then, that it has been used as a double for tropical climes in advertisements.

It was long thought that pirates had brought the palms to Crete. It was said they hid here after their raids, and that the palm grove grew from the discarded stones of the dates they had eaten. This story has since been disproved, but no matter how it was formed: Vai beach, with its palm grove, is a touristic highlight on Crete. In the 1970s this verdant natural attraction became especially popular with backpackers, today the bay is populated mainly by families and tourists taking selfies.

A large part of the roughly 20-hectare palm forest is now cut off by a fence, and a protected nature reserve, so that the natural beauty of Vai is preserved. In this way, the Cretan authorities seek to guarantee that visitors can still experience Caribbean flair in the middle of Europe for decades to come.

Address Epar.Od. Monis Toplous, Vai, 72300 Crete, Greece | Getting there By plane to Sitia, from there Vai beach is around 25 kilometres by car or bus | Tip To the right of the beach is a path leading to an observation platform, around a 10-minute walk away, that offers a panoramic view of the beach and palm grove.

22___ Christ Church Cathedral

The church with the most free-swinging bells

When the bells of Dublin's Christ Church Cathedral ring at 10am on Sunday morning, it comes on the back of a small feat of strength: the 19 bells of the medieval church are still rung by hand, and it's very physical work: the heaviest bell in Christ Church Cathedral weighs more than 2,000 kilograms.

The bells require 19 ringers, as each and every one is individually rung from the ringing chamber by means of its own rope. Like in an orchestra, the sequence of the bells is all about perfect timing and precise tuning, so that the end result is a harmonious ensemble rather than a discordant cacophony!

The cathedral, located in the heart of the Irish capital, was already an important pilgrimage site in the Middle Ages, and elaborate bell ringing has been part of church services for centuries. Each of the 19 bells is attached to its own wooden wheel and set in motion, back and forth, by the use of a rope, ultimately turning through 360 degrees. It is at the moment when a bell is vertical – at which point it is said to be 'on its head' – that the clapper touches the body and each bell creates a unique, tuned ringing. The interplay of all the bells and their different tunings enables the performance of complex tunes. This tradition, which is particularly widespread in Anglo Saxon countries, is called change ringing. There are around 5,000 churches with change ringing in England alone. It takes months or even years of practice before a bell-ringer is able to master the technique perfectly. There are even championships in change ringing.

But it's not only the bells that make Christ Church Cathedral worth a visit. Large, coloured windows flood the interior with a special light, and under the detailed floor mosaics lies one of the largest crypts in the country. This cathedral in Dublin is a wonderful environment that stimulates all of the senses.

Address Christchurch Place, Dublin 8, Ireland | **Getting there** Train to Dublin Heuston or Connolly Station, from there by bus: the nearest stops are High Street, Patrick Street and Lord Edward Street | **Hours** Daily apart from 26 Dec; find more information at www.christchurchcathedral.ie | **Tip** On a tour of the church, visitors can have a go at the change ringing technique for themselves.

23 — Tara River Canyon
The deepest canyon

The view from the Đurđevića-Tara bridge is one of a kind. Even up here, 150 metres in the air, you can hear the rumble of the Tara River as it flows under the bridge, clear, blue and wild. For thousands of years the river has channelled its way through nature. The water has doggedly cut a route through the massive rocks, creating an enormous canyon in the middle of a still largely untouched natural landscape.

Those who wish to discover the Tara River Canyon must travel to Montenegro. All around the mountain range in the north of the country lies the Durmitor National Park. At 59 kilometres in length, the country's longest river – the Tara – traverses the park. Steep walls of rock rise up almost vertically in the air on both banks, reaching up to 1,300 metres.

The region is a paradise for nature lovers and fans of extreme sports. The best way to explore the Tara River Canyon is on a rafting excursion. Depending on the water level, the trip downriver in a raft is sometimes leisurely, sometimes fast and furious. There are up to 40 rapids to master along the river. It is easiest in summer, when the Tara does not carry so much water. This is also the best time to begin the adventure if you don't have a high level of previous knowledge and want to enjoy the beauty of nature along the Tara in peace. It's certainly worth it, as the river leads past waterfalls that are up to 60 metres high and overgrown green riverbanks, past impressive rock formations and lots of small and large caves.

Those who dare can also chance a jump into the mostly crystal-clear water of the Tara and go for a swim. A test of courage that is not to be underestimated, as even in high summer the water rarely warms up to more than 12 °C. Even without this cold shock, a trip through the Tara River Canyon is a unique experience that's sure to make the heart of most visitors beat a little faster.

Address Durmitor National Park, 84220 Žabljak, Montenegro | Getting there From the capital of Montenegro, Podgorica, it's around 150 kilometres by car to the national park. Most rafting tours start in Žabljak. | Tip Right next to the Đurđevića-Tara bridge you can also cross the Tara River Canyon on a 350-metre zip-line (open mid-Apr–Oct).

24__Ice Music Festival
The coldest music festival

Crystal clear bell tones pair with the rhythmic sound of a marimba, followed by a scratching and scraping, then finally the deep, poignant sound of a horn. Can ice sound like this? It is a celestial soundtrack that fits perfectly with the ice-covered landscape around Finse. Once a year, the small Norwegian town becomes the setting for a very special music festival: with music played on instruments made of ice!

The musicians 'build' their instruments within a few hours, using blocks of ice extracted from the nearby lake. They fashion the ice into the required shape with chainsaws, planes and blowtorches. Not only must the sound of the instruments be right, but also their structure: if they are too delicate then they will break easily when being played. There isn't much time for the participants to practice, however, as the instruments begin to melt as soon as they start to play. Consequently, the musicians have to stay on their toes, and the key word that can be used to describe the performance is 'improvisation'!

That such a festival exists is thanks to Norwegian musician, Terje Isungset. He experimented early on with natural materials such as wood and stone, and a visit to an ice cave inspired him to explore its sonic potential. Isungset's explorations in icy sound have since developed into an entire music festival.

People from all around the world visit Norway for the frosty event, which takes place over several days every February, in order to experience the unique concerts. And they certainly are an experience, as not only the instruments, but also the stage and auditorium are made entirely of ice. As a consequence, musicians and audience sit outside in the middle of a wintery landscape, with temperatures that can fall to minus 20 °C or below. The event is a challenge, but the harmony of music and nature engenders great fascination in all involved.

Address 5719 Finse, Norway | **Getting there** Reach Finse by train in around 2.5 hours from Bergen, from Oslo in around four hours. | **Hours** Several days at the start of February | **Tip** The nearby glacier, Hardangerjøkul, which you can explore on guided hikes, served as a location for the ice planet Hoth in *Star Wars: Episode V – The Empire Strikes Back*.

25 Labirinto della Masone
The biggest bamboo labyrinth

Franco Maria Ricci actually studied geology, but the natural sciences were unable to thrill the scion of an aristocratic family from Parma for long. His heart, and his passion, belonged to the fine arts, to which he came to dedicate his life. Whether as graphic designer, publisher or art collector, this multi-talented man creatively lived out his interest in many areas. In 2003, he finally sold his publishing business in order to fulfil a life-long dream: the creation of the largest labyrinth in the world.

It was constructed on his property near Fontanellato, around 20 kilometres from Parma. Covering an area of 70,000 square metres, it was grown from around 200,000 bamboo plants. These Asian plants were perfect for his plans: stable, elegant and evergreen, and with an additional benefit: bamboo grows very quickly. The latter represented a particular advantage, as the former publisher was almost 70 years old when he began his project in 2005, and it took less than three years to bring the labyrinth into being.

The form of the maze is based on Roman mosaics. A system of paths totalling three kilometres in length leads through the bamboo maze. There are no curves or winding paths, only right angles. In this way, the three-metre-wide aisles all look the same, which guarantees that visitors – surrounded by metre-tall walls of green – will lose their way.

Those who ultimately make their way out of the labyrinth will find further insights into the late Signore Ricci's mind waiting for them inside the property. Alongside a library with all the works he published, a museum exhibits the patron's extensive private art collection. There are also rooms for exhibitions and concerts. This is unmistakably Ricci's life's work and his legacy: a place offering visitors the opportunity to lose themselves – both in the labyrinth, and in the arts.

Address Str. Masone 121, 43012 Fontanellato, Italy | Getting there By train to Fidenza or Parma, then around 15 minutes by car to the estate | Hours Apr–Oct 10.30am–7.30pm, Nov–Mar 9.30am–6.30pm; closed on Tue, 25 December and 1 January | Tip Castello Rocca Sanvitale in Fontanellato, with its frescoes by the Italian artist Parmigianino from the early 16th century, is also worth seeing.

26 Upper Rock Nature Reserve

The only wild monkeys

The British overseas territory of Gibraltar on the southern tip of Spain is a strange little place whichever way you look at it. A piece of Great Britain has been upheld here for more than 300 years, blessed with the Mediterranean climate and surrounded by Andalusian flair, where flamenco and sherry play the main parts. With tea time, red telephone boxes and a nice pint on an evening out at the pub, this is a little bit of England on less than seven square kilometres of land.

That alone would be reason enough to visit, but the main tourist magnet in Gibraltar is the Barbary apes, around 260 of which live on the small peninsula. They are actually native to North Africa, and it is suspected that they found their way to Gibraltar during Arabian rule in Spain from the eighth century onwards. In 1713, the contested rocks of Gibraltar were given to the British, and later became a Crown Colony. Today, it is the only place in Europe where the primates live in the wild.

They gambol about on the Upper Rock, with the rocks part of a protected nature reserve. If you want to see the Barbary apes you have to scale the 400-metre mountain, either on foot or by cable car. The animals usually don't leave visitors alone for long, as these cheeky monkeys worked out long ago that they can wrangle snacks from tourists. However, they all too often become more brazen than visitors feel comfortable with. Feeding is therefore strictly forbidden, and punished with heavy fines. This is mostly to protect the animals, as the monkeys often suffer from illnesses such as diabetes or caries.

Gibraltar is a unique case in Europe. Disputes over the sovereignty of the region erupt time and again between the UK and Spain, but the British are self-assured – even in the wake of Brexit. According to legend, their rule will last as long as there are monkeys on the rocks.

Address Upper Rock Nature Reserve, GX11 1AA, Gibraltar | **Getting there** Fly from the UK or Morocco, or arrive by land from the Spanish city of La Línea de la Concepcion. | **Hours** Daily 9.30am–7.15pm | **Tip** Even if you don't visit Gibraltar for the monkeys, it's worth entering the nature park. Short hikes are available on several routes, and when the weather's good it's possible to see all the way to Morocco, around 25 kilometres away.

27__Valle de Agaete

The only coffee-growing region

It is thought that it was a shepherd in the region of today's Ethiopia who discovered the coffee plant. He had observed that some of his goats leapt around wildly after they had eaten from the red fruit of the plant. This was a coincidence that laid the foundations for the creation of one of the most popular drinks in the world today, and the multi-billion dollar industry that surrounds it.

A particularly large amount of coffee is consumed in European countries, above all in Finland. Every Finn uses up an average of around 12 kilograms a year – that's three to four cups a day. Coffee is also the number one favourite drink in Germany, even ahead of water and beer. But the plants are grown in other parts of the world, with countries such as Brazil, Columbia, Indonesia and Ethiopia all known for their coffee production.

Few people know that there are also regions in Europe where coffee plants grow: in the mild climate of the Azores and the Canary Islands. Here some inhabitants have coffee plants in their own gardens and harvest the beans for their private consumption. Europe's largest growing region – and the only really commercial one – is located on Gran Canaria.

The Spanish island off the coast of North Africa offers the perfect conditions: mild temperatures throughout the year, and fertile lava soils. Consequently, coffee thrives amidst the lush vegetation in the elongated Valle de Agaete valley. Between 1,500 and 2,000 kilograms of coffee are produced here every year, under the motto 'small is beautiful'. The coffee beans are harvested by hand, and only the ripe, red fruit lands on the drying screen. Gran Canaria's coffee farmers also undertake further processing all the way to roasting directly on-site. The coffee from Agaete is not exported, and visiting coffee-lovers can get something here that's a real rarity in Europe: a regionally-grown cup of Joe.

Address Valle de Agaete, Province of Las Palmas, Gran Canaria, Spain | Getting there From Las Palmas de Gran Canaria it's around 30 kilometres to Agaete by bus or rental car. | Tip Harvest time is from March to June. Some fincas offer guided tours during which visitors can learn about coffee growing.

28 Excalibur

The tallest climbing tower

It is a characteristic that is even present in the name of the country: the Netherlands is flat. Open polders, wide fields of flowers and mud flats characterise the view no matter where you look. Around half of the small Western European state is less than one metre above sea level – and a quarter is even below it. The highest elevation in the Netherlands measures only 320 metres.

But precisely this absence of mountains has clearly triggered a yearning in some locals. While some dream of exotic tropical islands, others dream of the mountains of the Swiss Alps or the gigantic peaks of the Himalayas. The Netherlands even has its own climbers' association. It is therefore not so surprising that the tallest artificial climbing tower on the continent has been built here, in the flattest country in Europe.

Located at the Bjoeks climbing centre in Groningen, the tower rises 37 metres into the sky – that is about as tall as a 10-storey building. It also has up to 11 metres of overhang, which represents an approximation of real alpine climbing conditions. Its creators have called it 'Excalibur', inspired by the famous sword belonging to the mythical King Arthur, and the form of the tower is reminiscent of the weapon embedded in the stone. According to the legend, the sword makes its holder invincible and gives them superhuman powers – perhaps that's how climbers are supposed to feel when making an ascent in Groningen!

Excalibur is definitely not for beginners, and only experienced sports people are allowed to attempt this challenging wall. Those who make it to the top are even allowed to spend the night on the tower's platform – well secured, of course. Bivouacking at such great height is a very special experience for fans of climbing. After spending the night outside they can enjoy the sunrise – and the view of the flat, wide-open landscape of the Netherlands.

Address Klimcentrum Bjoeks, Bieskemaar 3, 9735 AE Groningen, The Netherlands | **Getting there** By train to Groningen, then by bus (lines 3 and 4) to P+R Kardinge | **Hours** Mon–Fri 2–11pm, Sat & Sun 11am–11pm | **Tip** The climbing centre is part of the large Kardinge sports park with various facilities. Those who don't want to climb, can swim or ice skate, or play tennis or ice hockey.

30__Hay-on-Wye
The first book village

It sounds a little bit like a story from one of the many books that are piled up to the ceiling in Richard Booth's shop: a businessman arrives in a remote Welsh village, buys an old castle, and pronounces himself king – or more precisely, ruler over the kingdom of books. But this is no fictional narrative. On the contrary, this is exactly what happened here in Hay-on-Wye.

Literature lover Richard Booth came from Oxford to this small village in the middle of nowhere, located on the border between Wales and England. In 1962 he opened his first antique book shop, followed by another a couple of years later. Business was good, and so the idea for a whole book village came into being: a place in which everything should just be about a love of literature. Enterprising locals carted used books into the 1,800-person village by the truck load – and Booth named himself king of the whole thing. It was a high-profile stunt that attracted a lot of visitors.

For a period of time a second-hand book shop was opened in every shop that became available, and there are currently 18 of them. These book emporiums have around 1.5 million books for sale on their shelves, in attics and cellar storage. Most of them are used, with their dog-eared pages and threadbare spines evidence of their earlier lives. While browsing, it's possible to find rarities that you won't find anywhere else. Some shopkeepers have specialised, for example in children's books, poetry, thrillers or guidebooks. There is also a literary festival every year at the end of May – start of June, which brings renowned authors into the Welsh province. Zadie Smith and Salman Rushdie are among the many famous writers who have read from their books here.

That Richard Booth once crowned himself king of the world's first book village had no legal ramifications. But it was the beginning of a great story.

Address Hay-on-Wye, Powys, Wales | **Getting there** From Cardiff by train to Hereford in England, from there, regular buses to Hay-on-Wye | **Tip** On the walls of the castle in Hay-on-Wye there's a very special second-hand bookshop with shelves in the open air: the Honesty Bookshop. All books cost £1, and payment is via an honesty box.

31__Heltermaa–Rohuküla
The longest ice road

Unfastening your seat belt is mandatory here! As crazy as it sounds, those who drive on Estonia's ice roads are subject to some unusual traffic regulations. In order to get out of the car quickly in an emergency, the otherwise obligatory seat belt represents an obstacle, and is thus forbidden.

Fortunately such emergencies are rare. The Estonian authorities keep a close eye on the network of ice roads, which is the only one of its kind in Europe. There are seven of these icy transport arteries in Estonia – given that the winter weather is cold enough, of course. The longest is around 26 kilometres long, and connects the town of Heltermaa on the Baltic island of Hiiumaa off the coast of Estonia with the harbour city of Rohuküla on the mainland. The ice road only opens when there have been weeks of freezing weather. The layer of ice must consistently be at least 25 centimetres thick. Only then can the inhabitants of the island begin to travel over the great white expanse.

There are special rules for doing so. Vehicles are only allowed on the ice during daylight hours, and only at a distance of one to two minutes from each other. In this way the fragile surface is not strained too heavily. There are also clear guidelines for speed: between 10 and 25 kilometres an hour, or 40 and 70, are allowed. Other speeds can be dangerous, as vehicles can create an effect that causes the ice sheet to vibrate, which in turn leads to cracks, and the potential for the ice to break.

For the residents of Hiiumaa, the opening of the ice road is always a major event – and an enormous blessing, as many of them work on the mainland. Instead of the almost one-and-a-half-hour ferry trip, they can reach Rohuküla by car in only 30 minutes. Crossing the frozen Baltic Sea this way is a special experience, and an impressive sight that can have vanished the next day in a thaw.

Address Heltermaa, Hiiumaa island, Estonia | Getting there From Tallinn reach the island of Hiiumaa by air, or by bus and ferry. From Heltermaa you can drive back to the mainland via the ice road. | Tip As soon as the Baltic Sea is frozen you can see ice sailors off Hiiumaa. The sport has a long tradition in Estonia. They race over the ice on runners at up to 100km/h, powered by the wind.

32 Suurhusen Church Tower

The farthest leaning tower

It certainly looks a bit silly when the tourists strain themselves in order to snap a funny holiday photo. They strike strange poses in front of the leaning tower of Pisa, to make it look as if they are holding it up. People have long since become used to this scene in the Italian city. The tower, which leans around four degrees to one side, is their emblem.

People in the small East Frisian village of Hinte can only smile at this. Here, on the most north-westerly tip of Germany, stands a tower that easily outshines its Italian counterpart. Suurhusen church tower boasts a lean of 5.19 degrees. As such, it is in fact the farthest leaning tower in the world – something confirmed by the *Guinness Book of Records*. At 27 metres in height, it bends almost two and a half metres to the side.

The building stood as straight as an arrow for centuries, and offered local residents sanctuary from the innumerable storm surges on the nearby North Sea. It was only in the 19th century that the heavy oak boards in the base of the 2,000-tonne tower slowly began to disintegrate. The rotten material yielded more and more under the tower's weight, and it gradually sank to the side. In 1970, the church had to be closed due to the danger of collapse, but the Suurhusen locals wanted to save their leaning tower. As a result, and with great commitment, the building was renovated. Eleven supports of reinforced concrete were anchored deep into the ground in order to stabilise the structure's foundations. Now church services can once again take place under the tilted steeple.

Entry in the *Guinness Book of Records* has brought many visitors to the East Frisian tower, but so far Suurhusen hasn't seen the huge droves of tourists who can be found almost every day in Pisa. As a result, if you're lucky, you might just have this particular world record holder all to yourself.

Address Am schiefen Turm 39, 26759 Hinte, Germany | Getting there From Bremen by train to Emden, then by bus (lines 410, 480) to Suurhusen church | Hours Guided tours Tue, Wed, Fri & Sat 10am–noon & 3.30–6pm (Apr–Oct), and by arrangement; more information at: www.kirche-suurhusen.de | Tip On important religious holidays there are services in the church. On selected dates the church band Schieflage ('Tilt') also plays.

33__Hum
The smallest city

According to the legend, it was giants who built this city on a hill in Istria. After they had constructed numerous impressive cities in the nearby Mirna valley, there were only a few stones remaining. They therefore decided to build a miniature city, and it was this that led to the creation of Hum: a city no bigger than a village, on an area around the size of half a football pitch, but nonetheless featuring a church tower, city wall and town hall.

Summer is high season in Hum. During this period the number of tourists who stroll through the twisting alleyways every day surpasses the number of residents many times over – and this isn't difficult, because only 28 people call the small settlement in western Croatia home. That Hum is even considered a city is a relic from the Middle Ages. Back then, it was bestowed a city charter as an economic and cultural centre.

Since that time Hum seems to have hardly changed in many respects. With its fortress-like walls and the historic stone houses, the place seems like the backdrop for a movie in a medieval setting. Glagolitic script, a Slavic alphabet from the early Middle Ages, was used here right up until the early 20th century, and Glagolitic writing can be seen on many walls in Hum to this day. The annual election of the mayor is also a rather old-fashioned affair. The citizens select their candidate by cutting a notch in a piece of wood. Whoever has notched up the most votes, literally, in the end, is bestowed the honorary post for the next year.

The recipe for the typical mistletoe schnapps, Biska, which is served in Hum's only tavern, is probably even older than this tradition. In ancient times the Celts are said to have valued it highly due to its alleged healing powers. The slightly bitter pomace brandy was apparently invented in Hum – yet another legend that makes Europe's smallest city a big attraction.

Address 52425 Hum, Istria, Croatia | **Getting there** By train or plane to Rijeka, then around one hour by car | **Tip** North of Hum is the village of Roč. From there, the Glagolitic Alley stretches to Hum. It is lined by 10 stone monuments to the development of the historical Glagolitic language. The city gates of Hum form the 11th and final station.

34 Mileștii Mici
The largest wine cellar

Needing a car in order to explore a wine cellar is rare, even for the most experienced and enthusiastic of wine connoisseurs. But on the Mileștii Mici estate, almost 20 kilometres south of the Moldovan capital, Chișinău, it is everyday life. The subterranean wine store is so vast that a visitor would only manage to see a tiny part of it without the use of motorised transport.

Barely to be suspected from the outside, the tunnel-like corridors of the wine cellar stretch over a total of 200 kilometres. As you travel through the seemingly endless underground labyrinth of barrels and tanks by car, you can make out road signs in the headlights. To make navigation easier, the paths are named after grape varieties.

The wine cellars of Mileștii Mici are housed in a former limestone mine. The humidity inside is between 85 and 95 per cent, while the temperature is at a stable 12–14 °C. Wealthy private customers from around the world rent space here in order to store their wine in these ideal conditions. But what the Moldovan vintner is most proud of is the vineyard's own 'golden collection': more than 1.5 million bottles of wine of different kinds, stored at a depth of around 80 metres. The oldest examples date from 1969, and many of the dusty bottles on the shelves are valuable rarities. It is the largest collection of wine in the world.

That the small republic of Moldova should become a place of superlative in all things wine-related is no coincidence. Wine has been produced around Mileștii Mici for as long as there have been people here, with a tradition of wine-growing in the former Soviet republic thanks to the fertile soils and the mild climate. The tiny country has more vineyards than all of the German wine-growing regions combined, but due to its sheer dimensions it will be quite a while before the largest wine cellar in Europe even approaches its maximum capacity.

Address 6819 Ialoveni, Moldova | Getting there The vineyard is around 30 minutes by car from the Moldovan capital, Chişinău. | Hours Mon–Fri 9am–5pm; guided tours must be booked | Tip If you want to take part in wine tasting, you should organise a taxi back to Chişinău: there is a zero-alcohol policy for driving in Moldova.

35 __ Sublimotion
The most expensive restaurant

Dignified atmosphere, elegant tablecloths and candlelight, some classical music playing softly in the background – you would normally expect all of this from dinner in an expensive restaurant. But you won't find any of it in Sublimotion on Ibiza – yet it still outshines the most classy of multi-starred restaurants in terms of price: the menu costs €1,650 per person. On a single evening here customers can end up handing over the kind of money that some people spend on an entire holiday. Nevertheless, the tables are mostly booked out far in advance, as Sublimotion does more than serve food.

The concept of the restaurant, which is housed in the Hard Rock Hotel on the Spanish holiday island, is extremely unusual. It is a mixture of culinary experience, art and interactive show. The only table in the restaurant seats a maximum of 12 guests. Each of the 20 courses served across the evening is thoroughly considered, right down to the smallest detail, with fitting sounds, elaborate projections on the walls or elements that guests experience through virtual-reality headsets.

If, for example, fish and seafood is served, the room transforms into a kind of underwater world. If mushrooms are the main ingredient for a course, guests will suddenly find themselves sitting in the middle of an illusionary autumnal forest. Even the aromas and humidity in the dining room are adjusted to make them relevant to the dish being served.

An experience for all the senses – that was the concept developed by chef and initiator, Paco Roncero. In order to make that a reality, the two-star chef added a film director, a composer and an illusion artist to his team, alongside some top chefs. The menu becomes a total artwork through the interplay of all the elements. However, the restaurant is only open in summer: the rest of the year the team are at work on striking new concepts for next season.

Address Ctra. Playa d'en Bossa s/n, Sant Jordi de ses Salines, 07817 Ibiza, Spain | Getting there The restaurant is part of the Hard Rock Hotel, and just a few kilometres from the capital of the island on the popular Playa d'en Bossa beach. | Hours June – Sept daily from 9pm; booking required | Tip Playa d'en Bossa is *the* party beach on Ibiza. If you still have some money left after visiting the restaurant, offload it in one of the many nightclubs.

36__Steinkaulenberg
The only gemstone mine

The great diamond fever has long left Idar-Oberstein. And yet still it glitters and sparkles all over. The city in south-west Germany is all about gemstones. Even though there has been no commercial prospecting here for around 150 years, the trade in jewels flourishes to this day nonetheless. Jewellery shops line the streets of the 30,000-resident city, and the traditional craft of gemstone cutting also continues to be practised in some of Idar-Oberstein's workshops. It is also home to the only gemstone mine in Europe that is open to visitors.

The mines of the Steinkaulenberg were plundered for agate, amethysts and rock crystal for around 400 years. Men mined the valuable stones from the hard rock by hand, using hammers and chisels. The heyday of prospecting in Idar-Oberstein was in the 17th and 18th centuries. Although the yield gradually declined and the mines were eventually closed, gemstone processing remained. These days, emeralds and diamonds are imported, in particular from South America, and refined here.

For around 40 years, tourists have had the chance to transport themselves back to the mining era. In the visitor gallery of the former mines it's possible to find out everything related to the creation of gemstones, and their origins of around 270 million years ago, when there was still strong volcanic activity in the region. As hot lava cooled down, air bubbles were formed, and gemstone crystals then developed inside these bubbles over millions of years, through the ingress of acids and sulphur compounds.

Quartzes and rock crystals still sparkle on the walls of the exhibition mine today, effectively illuminated by spotlights. You can even try your luck on the mine's former spoils heap. In this way, the occasional precious discovery travels back home with a lucky visitor, a very special souvenir from Idar-Oberstein.

Address Im Stäbel, 55743 Idar-Oberstein, Germany | Getting there By rail from Frankfurt am Main to Idar-Oberstein, then bus 330 or 332 to Mackenrodter Weg near the gemstone mine | Hours Daily 10am–5pm, 15 Mar–30 Nov | Tip There are more than 10,000 valuable objects exhibited in the Deutsches Edelsteinmuseum in Idar-Oberstein. It is directly opposite the gemstone exchange, the city's most important trading place.

37_Kapalı Çarşı
The biggest bazaar

It feels like a city within the city. 21 gates lead into the Kapalı Çarşı, Istanbul's 'covered market'. Inside, there's an endless jumble of voices and aromas, people and goods. On many corners the scent of cloves, cinnamon and cardamom hangs in the air. More than 3,600 shops huddle alongside each other in the 65 alleys and streets of the bazaar. From carpets and leather goods, via spices and teas, to ornately decorated lamps and jewellery, it's possible to find pretty much anything your heart desires here.

The Kapalı Çarşı is located in the historic Istanbul district of Eminönü, not far from the famous Hagia Sophia. Up until the middle of the 15th century, this was the largest church in Christendom. When Sultan Mehmet II conquered what was then Constantinople, he converted it into the main mosque of the metropolis on the Bosporus. In the following years he had the big bazaar constructed very close by.

The market was originally built of wood, but was replaced by a stone construction following several fires. The striking architecture – alongside the variety of goods – impresses visitors to this day. Skilfully painted stone arches stretch above the colourful chaos of the market's hustle and bustle. Alongside shops and restaurants, visitors can also find mosques, impressive marble fountains and hammams under the vaulted ceilings.

It isn't hard to get lost in the maze of alleys, even though most of the streets are named after the particular trade whose products are on offer, so if you're visiting Kapalı Çarşı for the first time, be sure to take a map! The most important thing you have to bring, however, is the ability to haggle, because one thing certainly hasn't changed over the centuries since it was built: the price is always patiently negotiated – a ritual that is as much part of Kapalı Çarşı as the Hagia Sophia is part of Istanbul.

Address Kalpakçılar Caddesi, Beyazıt, 34126 Istanbul, Turkey | Getting there From Marmaray Sirkeci İstasyonu railway station by tram T1 to Beyazıt, then the Kapalı Çarşı can be reached on foot | Hours Mon–Sat 8.30am–7pm | Tip If you like things even more exotic, you should visit Mısır Çarşısı, the Egyptian bazaar, only 10 minutes' walk away. The main products on sale here are teas and spices, which attract customers with their bright colours and intense aromas.

38 Dettifoss
The most powerful waterfall

You can already hear the roar of the water from some way away, like a goods train rushing past in the distance. Clouds of tiny water droplets rise up above the chasm and lie over the landscape like wafts of mist. The closer you get, the louder and wetter it becomes. Dettifoss is the most powerful waterfall in Europe. Every second, more than 190 cubic metres of water plunge untamed into the depths, at a width of around 100 metres. This is impressive proof of the power of nature, in the middle of the rugged north-eastern area of Iceland.

The Dettifoss stands for this region of the island, which is still largely untouched and sparsely populated, like an allegory. Here it is still possible to experience the wild beauty of Iceland in an almost pure form. The river Jökulsá á Fjöllum channels its way through this jagged landscape, fed by Iceland's largest glacier, Vatnajökull. Stones and scree are carried in the meltwater, and give the river a menacing dark colour.

Around 30 kilometres before it reaches the Arctic Ocean, Jökulsá á Fjöllum pours into an almost 45-metre-deep canyon, and forms the Dettifoss, which translates as 'collapsing waterfall'. A narrow footpath leads to the break-off edge. From there, enveloped in the spray from the Dettifoss, visitors can see the masses of grey-brown water rumbling into the depths, before it continues its way through the Jökulsárgljúfur canyon.

Hollywood directors have already discovered the impressive landscape around the powerful waterfall, and used it as a backdrop. Ridley Scott, for example, filmed the opening scene of his science-fiction film *Prometheus* here, while Tom Cruise stood in front of the camera in this location for the post-apocalyptic spectacle *Oblivion*. Where else could you stage such a visually stunning 'end of the world' scenario as in the middle of pristine nature on the outer edge of Iceland?

Address Jökulsárgljúfur National Park, Iceland | Getting there It's around a seven-hour drive from Reykjavík to Dettifoss, while it takes around two hours from Akureyri, the biggest city in the north of Iceland. | Tip You can reach two more waterfalls walking from Dettifoss along the Jökulsá á Fjöllum. One kilometre upstream is the Selfoss, while two kilometres downstream is Hafragilsfoss. Both are less violent, but equally worth seeing.

39___Icehotel
The oldest ice hotel

A visit to an ice hotel isn't exactly the first choice for people who prefer to spend their holidays under palm trees in warmer climes. But if you can manage to overcome your fear of freezing, you'll be rewarded with a unique natural experience. Visitors to this hotel spend the night amid ice and snow around 200 kilometres north of the Arctic Circle, in the Swedish locality of Jukkasjärvi.

Everything began in 1989, with an exhibition of ice art. A large igloo was created as the exhibition space for the cold creations. A short time later people wanted to spend the night in the icy atmosphere, and thus the idea of an ice hotel developed. The project grew bigger and bigger, but the artistic approach remained. Icehotel is today not only the oldest establishment of its kind, but also a huge art gallery. Every room has its own motto. Artists from all around the world transform the frosty bed chambers into elaborately designed suites with ice sculptures and other creative details – every winter anew.

The work begins in November, when the temperatures in Jukkasjärvi drop ever lower. The 'building material' for the unusual hotel comes from the frozen river Torne, with extremely heavy blocks of ice used in the construction. Mixed with snow, they become Icehotel's walls, beds and sculptures. Alongside the actual hotel rooms, a hotel lobby, a bar and a church are also made this way. Like in a classic igloo, the dome-shaped structures are self-supporting.

The thick walls of ice and snow insulate the rooms. As a result, even if the temperatures outside sink to minus 30 °C, it stays at minus five inside – small mercies! In order for them to weather the night in this ice-cold setting in relative comfort, visitors are given especially warm sleeping bags. And for those who are still cold, there's always the house recipe for warming you up: a hot glass of cranberry juice.

Address Marknadsvägen 63, 98191 Jukkasjärvi, Sweden | Getting there Train or plane to Kiruna, then to the hotel by bus, taxi or dogsled | Hours Dec–Apr; an offshoot, Icehotel 365, is open all year round – cooled by energy generated via solar panels in the roof | Tip Observe the Northern Lights near Jukkasjärvi on a snowmobile tour, available mid-December to mid-April.

40___Júzcar
The only blue village

The '*pueblos blancos*', the white villages in the hinterland of Andalusia, are well known. They are among the most popular sights of the region in southern Spain. Júzcar was also one of these white villages until a few years ago, but relatively few tourists strayed this way. The 230-person village in one of the more remote areas of the province of Málaga was for a long time a sleepy mountain village.

Everything changed in 2011, however – suddenly the whole place shone in radiant sky blue. The reason for this was an advertising campaign, which saw Júzcar transformed into a lifelike Smurf Village for the premiere of the new 3D film *The Smurfs*. Thanks to 9,000 litres of paint and many helping hands, facade after facade was painted the distinctive shade. Every house, every shop, even the town hall, the church and the cemetery was given a new, Smurf-like colour. The stunt was a complete success, and many people visited Júzcar for the premiere party.

Six months later the village was actually supposed to be restored to its original condition, but by this time the residents had become used to the new colour scheme and the unexpected attention it generated. As a result, a ballot was held, and the majority of the inhabitants decided to keep the village in its new colour. Since then, Júzcar has been known as Smurf Village.

Many house walls are lovingly decorated with Smurf motifs, you can have your photograph taken with a larger-than-life Papa Smurf, or visit the blue market. There are also extra attractions, such as make-up stands or crafting tables, especially at the weekend – all perfectly matched to the universe of the pointy-hatted gnomes.

The comic figures by Belgian cartoonist Peyo made their first appearance in 1958. Surely, he could never, in his wildest dreams, have predicted that a real Smurf Village would be created in the middle of Andalusia more than 50 years later.

Address Júzcar, Province of Málaga, Spain | Getting there The best way to reach the village is by car (about 60 kilometres from Marbella). | Tip You'll get the best view of the blue village from Mirador de la Torrichela.

41__Kalmykia
The only Buddhist region

The nine-metre-tall statue of Buddha sits before you, impressive and shiny. The fragrance of smouldering joss sticks hangs in the air, while in the background there is the constant murmur of the monks reciting their mantras. When you experience a ceremony in the Golden Temple of Elista, you'd be forgiven for believing that you're no longer in Europe – but you definitely haven't left the continent.

Elista is the capital of Kalmykia. The autonomous federal republic of Russia lies between the Caucasus and Caspian Sea in the southern Russian steppes, and geographically is part of Europe. It is the only mainly Buddhist region – a piece of Asia on the European continent. The Kalmyk nomads, a Mongol subgroup, came here around 400 years ago. They brought their faith with them from Asia, and have held on to it since then, even though this wasn't always easy over the course of history.

The republic was dissolved in 1943 under the reign of Stalin, spiritual leaders were persecuted, and the temples destroyed. The entire Kalmyk people were deported to Siberia, and only allowed to return to the region after the end of Stalinism. Since the fall of the Soviet Union in 1990, Buddhism has flourished again in Kalmykia. There are now temples, pagodas and religious statues everywhere, especially in the capital city of Elista.

Around 160,000 of the almost 300,000 Kalmyks are Buddhist. Their spiritual centre is the Golden Temple in Elista, which was opened in 2005. The Dalai Lama himself chose its location on a visit. At nine metres, the temple's statue of Buddha is the tallest in Europe. The Golden Temple also houses a museum, in which the Buddhist traditions of the Kalmyks are illuminated. The entire temple complex is open to visitors, which means that non-Buddhists can also turn the prayer wheel and try to get a bit closer to the meaning of life: happiness and contentment.

Address Republic of Kalmykia, Russia | **Getting there** By plane via Moscow to Elista | **Tip** Play chess on the central Lenin Square in Elista in the evening. Chess is Kalmykia's national sport, and in many places there are large public chess boards where people play.

42 Pyramidenkogel
The tallest wooden observation tower

Glamorous villas and small castles nestle on the banks of the turquoise-coloured Wörthersee. The region, embedded in the lush green landscape of the Austrian state of Carinthia, is characterised by late-19th and early 20th-century architecture. The roughly 850-metre mountain of Pyramidenkogel, with its observation tower, looms up in the middle of it all, on the Wörthersee's south bank.

The futuristic construction of wood and steel seems alien amidst the beauty of nature. 16 larch wood supports screw up into the sky, and form the outer sheath of this unusual structure. Inside, diagonal steel braces ensure the stability of the tower, which is 100 metres from ground to tip. There are three viewing platforms, the highest of which is at around 70 metres: more than enough for a unique outlook. In good weather you can make out the mountains of Slovenia in the south, while the Wörthersee gleams to the north.

The wide panorama was already being enjoyed here in 1950, the year the first wooden viewing tower on the Pyramidenkogel was built. It held up against the changing weather conditions for almost 20 years. Its successor was built from reinforced concrete, but over time the material also deteriorated, until the tower eventually had to be demolished. The modern construction, with its striking architecture, followed in 2012.

If you want to reach the highest platform, you'll have to climb exactly 441 steps – or take the panorama lift. There's an alternative route back for the courageous: a slide from half way up. This closed pipe allows daring visitors to go spiralling down at speeds of up to 25 kilometres an hour. During the summer it's possible to speed back down to the ground on a zip line, too. Regardless of which method you choose, once you're safely on terra firma, the route is the same for everyone: back through the forested hills of Carinthia towards the turquoise Wörthersee.

Address Pyramidenkogel, Linden 62, 9074 Keutschach am See, Austria | **Getting there** Train to Klagenfurt, or bus 5310 or 5316 to Reifnitz, then line 5314 to Pyramidenkogel | **Hours** Varies according to season, more information at www.pyramidenkogel.info | **Tip** Enjoy the landscape on a boat trip on the Wörthersee. You can reach the Pyramidenkogel by foot from the pier in Reifnitz in around 1.5 hours.

43 Arsenalna
The deepest underground station

You certainly need a bit of patience, as it takes around five minutes to get from the top to the platform of Arsenalna metro station. That's because it's around 105 metres beneath the surface – so deep that the escalator had to be split. It leads the passengers in its two sections into the depths of the Ukrainian capital, to the stop on metro line 1.

Plans for a metro in Kiev already existed at the end of the 19th century, but it took until 1960 before the first section of track could be opened. This included Arsenalna station. As the entrance is located on a group of hills, the engineers were forced to drill especially far into the earth. Kiev's sandy soil and the abundance of water in the river Dnepr, which traverses the city, represented a challenge for the architects. During construction, parts of the ground were artificially frozen in order to stabilise it for drilling. It was 11 years until the first section of the city's metro, 5.4 kilometres long, was finally finished.

Today, the route network of the Kiev metro is around 70 kilometres long, and comprises 52 stations. Three of these, including Arsenalna, are now protected historical structures. Their architecture reflects the style of Socialist Classicism: prestigious, weighty and ornate. The underground stations of the former Soviet republics were supposed to be 'palaces of the working class'. This was also the case for Arsenalna station, built near the strategically important arsenal factory. 10,000 workers were employed in the production of optical devices here after World War II – including for the military and Soviet aerospace industry. After work, they would be greeted by an impressive domed hall upon entering the metro station, with marble and red granite on the walls. At the time, the Kiev metro was seen as a symbol of progress. Today, it is one of the city's best-known sights.

Address Ivana Mazepy St., Kiev, 0200 Ukraine | Getting there From the main station there is a direct connection to the Arsenalna station on metro line 1. | Hours Daily 6am–midnight | Tip It's just a few minutes' walk from the metro station to Mariyinsky Park, where you can view the impressive Mariyinsky Palace, the official residence of the Ukrainian President.

44__Dyrehavsbakken
The oldest amusement park

First you hear the incessant wooden clattering, as the 'Rutscheba-nen' struggles its way up to around 20 metres. Then you see it race downhill at great speed, as the old lady, dating back to 1932, manages an impressive 75 kilometres an hour. The 'Rutschebanen' is one of the oldest wooden rollercoasters in the world – and one of the main attractions of the Dyrehavsbakken amusement park north of Copenhagen.

'Bakken', as the locals usually call it, is not nearly as well known as Tivoli in the heart of the Danish capital, despite being quite a bit older. And it is precisely its age that makes the atmosphere special. Many of the rides and stalls radiate a nostalgic charm. There are no neon light advertisements or sales stands from large chains to be found here. Independent showmen and business people run most of the attractions – and that is related to the park's genesis.

In 1583, a water spring was discovered in the woods near the city of Copenhagen, which was soon said to have healing powers. Many people made a pilgrimage here as a result. Over the course of time the stream of visitors also attracted vendors, offering drinks and food. They were followed in turn by jugglers, who hoped for a few coins for the art they performed. Soon acrobats, actors and bear tamers guaranteed a colourful and varied programme of entertainment. The plot became a popular destination for trips out of the city, and the showmen eventually formed an association, the main features of which survive to this day.

Of course there are now modern attractions at 'Bakken' alongside the historic fairground rides. Wild rides in spinning gondolas, a 5D cinema or a driving simulator ensure the typical amusement park flair, but the spirit of yesteryear is ever-present. By the time you climb aboard the wooden 'Rutschebanen', you'll be setting off on a trip into another era.

Address Dyrehavevej 61, 2930 Klampenborg, Denmark | Getting there Take the suburban train to Klampenborg from the centre of Copenhagen. | Hours Mid-Apr–mid-Sept daily from 1pm, extra opening hours in the Danish autumn holidays and on Advent weekends | Tip The 'Bakken' is surrounded by the forest of the royal park Jægersborg Dyrehave. From Klampenborg station you can take a coach ride through the park.

45 — Kopaonik Ski Resort
The longest artificial ski slope

You couldn't really complain about there being too few tourists in Kopaonik. Serbia's oldest and largest ski resort is extraordinarily popular among locals and visitors from the Balkans and Russia. The gentle mountains of the Kopaonik range are located in the far south of the country. Even during the Kosovo conflict, when war was raging through the entire region, the hotels here were fully booked, and the ski lifts continued to whirr, conveying passengers to the top of the slopes.

In recent years, Kopaonik has experienced yet another boom. The number of classy hotels and modern chairlifts has mushroomed. Queues of skiers and snowboarders regularly form at the valley stations, waiting to explore the 55 kilometres of pistes. At an altitude of around 1,700 metres, the town is therefore often dubbed 'Serbia's St Moritz'. Perhaps it was this popularity that led to the decision to extend the ski season beyond the winter months. As a result, it's now possible to ski down the mountains when the hills all around are lush with green foliage – on an artificial slope.

The route is 800 metres long, and covers around 115 metres of elevation. Mats of synthetic material make this possible. These dry slopes have a special surface, over which skis glide almost as well as over real snow. Dark green with signal red edges, they form an unfamiliar sight in the middle of the Serbian mountain landscape. The plastic pistes are said to last for at least 10 years, after which they will be recycled.

Thanks to the installation of these artificial ski slopes it is now quite normal to see people in T-shirts and shorts, equipped with skis and helmets, making their way into the mountains of Kopaonik in mid-summer. This kind of downhill skiing may not appeal to those dyed-in-the-wool winter sports fans, but certainly provides welcome variety for visitors during the warmer months of the year.

Address 36354 Kopaonik, Serbia | Getting there From Belgrade it's around four hours by car or bus to Kopaonik. | Tip Top Serbian tennis player, Novak Đoković, is from near Kopaonik, and learned to ski here. With a bit of luck you might spot the elite sportsman on the piste or enjoying the après-ski.

46 La Gomera

The only place whistling is a language at school

La Gomera is the second-smallest of the Canary Islands. The volcanic island, which like all of the Canaries is under the dominion of Spain, is geographically small, at only 22 kilometres long and 25 kilometres wide. But if you think that means you can travel between places quickly, then you're mistaken. La Gomera is made up mainly of tall mountains and deep gorges, with innumerable serpentine roads winding through the island's rugged landscape. It's no surprise, then, that a special form of communication has developed here: the whistling language called Silbo Gomero.

At a time when mobile phones or even landlines remained far off in the future, messages could be conveyed across deep valleys and information exchanged by using whistles. Even the indigenous people of the island are thought to have communicated this way. And while similar whistling languages have almost died out in other regions of Europe, the tradition is kept alive on La Gomera. For around 20 years, Silbo Gomero has been a compulsory subject in all schools on the island. And since 2009, the language has been a UNESCO Intangible Cultural Heritage.

The communication system is made up of only six whistle sounds: four consonants and two vowels. But that doesn't mean it is easy, as an astonishing amount of around 4,000 terms can be covered with this limited range of sounds, depending on sequence, volume and pitch. The precise meaning of a message is usually revealed through its context. When conditions are good, the whistles can be heard from up to three kilometres away.

Many islanders use the language regularly to this day. They can even identify the person with whom they are communicating by the sound of their whistle: just like the human voice, the whistle of each person is unique. Silbo Gomero is a cultural relic that not only has a past, but also a future, thanks to school lessons on La Gomera.

Address La Gomera, Canary Islands, Spain | Getting there By plane to Tenerife South, then taxi or bus to Los Cristianos; from there the ferry departs to La Gomera | Tip In the Garajonay National Park in the centre of the island, at the Mirador de Igualero viewing point, there's a memorial for Silbo Gomero. The modern sculpture symbolises a whistling islander.

47 Museo Atlántico

The first underwater museum

A boat takes you from the southern tip of Lanzarote to Las Coloradas bay, which is located around 10 minutes away. Here, off the coast of the Canary Island, is an unusual art exhibition. The 'Museo Atlántico' is located at a depth of around 14 metres, with almost 300 large-format sculptures installed on the sea floor over an area of 2,500 square metres. If you want to see them, you have to dive into the underwater world of the Atlantic Ocean.

It is the work of a single artist: the Brit Jason deCaires Taylor has been creating the extraordinary sculpture park since 2016. His life-sized figures are modelled on real people. The extremely heavy works are created on land using pH-neutral cement, before being installed in their respective places on the sea floor. The surface of the sculptures is made in such a way that corals and other marine life settle on them. For the artist, it is also about giving something back to the seas that have been damaged by human and environmental factors. In this way, his underwater art will become an artificial reef, and thus a new habitat for fish and other marine animals over the course of time.

Encountering these motionless figures when diving off Lanzarote feels a little spooky. Many of the pieces address current issues. A faceless sculpture couple take selfies, then a little further on you swim over a dinghy, in which men, women and children are sitting tightly packed together. The latter piece, entitled *Raft of Lampedusa*, is intended to encourage reflection on the refugee crisis happening in the Mediterranean.

You can't admire the sculptures unless you possess a diving licence, but that doesn't bother Jason deCaires Taylor. After all, his art is not only made for humans. Seaweed and small corals are already starting to populate many of his figures, and cover the once grey concrete surfaces. Nature conquers his art – thus completing it.

Address 35580 Playa Blanca, Lanzarote, Spain | Getting there By plane to Arrecife, then rental car to Playa Blanca (around 30 kilometres), where diving trips to Museo Atlántico are available | Tip Only a few kilometres to the east of Playa Blanca are the Playas de Papagayo: small bays with fine sandy beaches and turquoise-coloured water.

48 Roque de los Muchachos Observatory
The largest reflecting telescope

The narrow road winds back and forth through more than 300 bends, up to 2,400 metres above sea level. Roque de los Muchachos is the tallest mountain on La Palma, and you will have long since left the tree line behind you when you see the telescopes in the distance, the spherical structures contrasting with their barren, rocky surroundings in bright white and silver.

Here, on the tiny Canary Island of La Palma, stands one of the largest observatories in the world. More than a dozen telescopes are scattered across the surrounding hills. Some stand open in the landscape and look like gigantic satellite dishes, others are protected under domes of varying sizes. Researchers use them to observe and assess distant planets, through which they seek to gain understanding of the formation of the universe.

On guided tours everyone can glean some insight into this world. The main attraction for visitors is the Gran Telescopio Canarias. At 10.4 metres in diameter, it is the largest optical reflecting telescope in Europe. When night falls, the 45-metre-tall dome opens up, and the telescope begins to collect valuable information about other galaxies. Black holes and exoplanets have already been discovered in this way.

Roque de los Muchachos on La Palma is the perfect location for the observatory. The Spanish island is located in the Atlantic several hundred kilometres from the mainland, and there is hardly any industry and no big cities here. Light pollution is therefore much less problematic than in most other places on the planet. In addition, the mountaintop is usually above the cloud base, thus enabling an unrestricted view. These are the best conditions for scientists and tourists alike to observe the sky in all its beauty, and wonder at what might exist in the heavens.

Address Roque de los Muchachos, 38728 La Palma, Spain | **Getting there** From La Palma airport by car towards Santa Cruz de La Palma, then around 1.5 hours on the LP-4 to Roque de los Muchachos. | **Hours** Guided tours daily; advance booking necessary – more information at www.iac.es | **Tip** Spread over the island is a whole network of 'astronomical viewing points', where it's possible to observe the firmament with the naked eye. Information panels help you identify the heavenly bodies and constellations.

49__Lake Ladoga
The biggest lake

When standing on the banks of Lake Ladoga, you'll often see nothing on the horizon but water. The freshwater lake in north-west Russia is simply enormous, at 220 kilometres long and up to 120 kilometres wide. It is an impressive inland sea, almost 35 times larger than Lake Constance. Surrounded by rugged banks and expansive woodlands, it seems as though the largest lake on the continent is far from civilisation – yet it is no more than 50 kilometres from St Petersburg.

Lake Ladoga is a popular local recreation area for city dwellers, especially in summer. Many have a dacha on the lake, and escape the hustle and bustle of the Russian metropolis here. They fish, swim, and enjoy the warm evenings with a view of the water and the more than 500 islands. Those who like to be a little more active can sail or watch lynxes and many species of bird while walking through the surrounding forests. With a little luck, if you take a canoe trip you might even see the ringed seals that live in the fresh water.

Those interested in culture will be drawn to the northern end of the lake, and the island of Walaam with its orthodox monastery. The first monks are thought to have settled here as far back as the 10th century. With an eventful history, and having been destroyed several times, the monastery is now an important pilgrimage site for orthodox Christians. The roughly 200 monks who live on the island are famous for their meditative singing. In winter, when the sea is not yet completely frozen, they are often cut off from the outside world for months on end.

Coming from St Petersburg to Lake Ladoga is like entering another world. A world shaped by nature and the seasons, in which it's possible to find peace and relaxation. Thanks to its enormous size, you can almost always find a spot where it seems as if you have the biggest lake in Europe completely to yourself.

Getting there From Finland Station in St Petersburg take the train to Ladoschkoje Osero on the south-west bank (around 1.5 hours) or the suburban railway Elektrischtka to Priosersk in the north-west of the lake (around 2.5 hours). | **Tip** You can also explore Lake Ladoga and the monastery island of Walaam by boat. This tour lasts several days, and starts in St Petersburg.

50 Liechtenstein

The only country to bear the name of a family

'Hoi metanand!' is the friendly greeting exchanged when people meet on one of Liechtenstein's many hiking routes, regardless of whether they know each other. Although it's quite possible they've already met in this small principality: only around 38,000 people live in the fourth-smallest country in Europe. The mini state in the Alps, bordered by Austria and Switzerland, is only 25 kilometres long, and a maximum of 12 kilometres wide.

The tiny principality has existed since 1719. Its destiny has been closely linked with the family that gave it its name: the Princely House of Liechtenstein. Their residence sits on a rocky terrace high above the capital city of Vaduz. But although at first sight the castle from the 12th century may seem to have been sealed off, the Princely family are considered down to earth and unpretentious. It is not rare to meet them on the street, greetings are exchanged, and perhaps a short chat. The noble offspring attend public schools. And on the annual national holiday in August, the prince invites the population for a drink in the private rose garden. Accessible aristocracy, one could say.

The fact that most of the citizens are financially well off surely adds to the relaxed atmosphere. Liechtenstein is after all one of the richest countries in the world. The economy is booming, there is almost 100 per cent employment, and Liechtenstein is one of very few states in the world that can claim to be debt-free.

If you wish to explore the prosperous principality as a tourist, you should do so on foot – along the Liechtenstein path, for example. This leads for 75 kilometres through all 11 of the country's municipalities, and past many important historical sites. Once you have walked along this hiking route you've basically seen the whole of Liechtenstein – and on the way certainly heard your fair share of 'Hoi metanand!'.

Getting there Liechtenstein can only be reached by land, e.g. by car from Zürich in Switzerland (110 kilometres) or from Innsbruck in Austria (170 kilometres). | Tip In the Schatzkammer Liechtenstein museum in Vaduz there are valuable weapons and works of art on display from the history of the principality – including the Ducal hat, with its 30 large and 99 small diamonds.

51 Braderie de Lille

The largest flea market

It is early on Saturday morning and the streets of Lille are already thronging with people. The merchants have spread out their wares on tables, sheets and covered stalls for potential customers to browse. The Braderie de Lille kicks off at 8am, beginning a marathon for lovers of antiques and bargain hunters alike. Every year on the first weekend in September, this city in northern France transforms into the biggest flea market in Europe, and in the process attracting in excess of two million visitors.

Around 10,000 dealers crowd on to a total of 100 kilometres of road in the old town of Lille. The vendors sell a huge variety of items, ranging from old furniture and vintage clothes to valuable paintings, historical jewellery and everything in between. The selection is huge! The streets of the city centre are veritably paved with used objects, and all around the atmosphere is celebratory, as numerous culinary specialities, art events and concerts are also undertaken.

The Braderie de Lille was first mentioned in writing back in 1127. At that time, valets were given the opportunity once a year to sell the old belongings and clothes of their wealthy masters. As a result, the second-hand goods market developed over the course of centuries, eventually becoming the large event that it is now. Today, the Braderie the Lille is not only a huge flea market, but also one of France's biggest fairs.

Where the name 'Braderie' comes from is not clear, however. One hypothesis is that it is derived from the Flemish word '*braaden*', which means 'roasting'. This could link it in with the most famous speciality, which is served here on every corner: Moules-frites – mussels with French fries. Around 500 tonnes of mussels are eaten in the city over the course of the weekend, with the shells piling up in small mountains on the pavements – yet another unique sight at the largest flea market in Europe.

Address Lille, Hauts-de-France, France | Getting there Train to Lille main station, then by foot or metro to the city centre | Tip For all sporty types, a half marathon takes place parallel to Braderie de Lille on the Saturday of the flea market weekend, with a route that passes many of the city's historic buildings.

52___Under

The first underwater restaurant

The food is of course exquisite, but when you book a table at Under, you're not only there for pleasant cuisine. A very special restaurant has been created in Lindesnes, on the sparsely populated southern tip of Norway. One that brings together gastronomy, architecture and science in a unique experience.

The ingredients for many of the dishes on the menu come from the restaurant's immediate surroundings: Under is located close to the coast, actually *in* the North Sea. The 1,600-tonne reinforced concrete building juts obliquely out of the water like a monolith that has accidentally slipped into the ocean. Only the smallest part of the 34-metre-long tube can be seen from the beach. A narrow jetty leads to the entrance of the modern structure, via which patrons descend into the dining room.

More than five metres under the surface of the sea, plain wooden tables are grouped in front of the restaurant's main attraction: a 40-square-metre panorama window. It dominates the room, which is flooded with blue-green sea light, like a cinema screen. Through the window you have a clear view of the underwater world off the Norwegian coast. Seaweed and kelp sway to the rhythm of the waves, and with a bit of luck you'll see larger fish such as pollack or cod, and sometimes even seals swimming past.

Scientists also make use of this window on to the underwater world. Under is not only a restaurant, but a research location too. Biologists study the behaviour of marine life here, taking advantage of the ideal conditions the building offers. The artificial light that shines through the glass attracts many fish and plankton. Cameras and measuring instruments are also mounted on the outer facade. Scientific research, tourist attraction and culinary pleasure go hand-in-hand at Under – the first underwater restaurant in Europe, that has given itself completely to the sea on so many levels.

Address Bålyveien 48, 4521 Lindesnes, Norway | **Getting there** Lindesnes is almost 400 kilometres from Oslo. The bus journey takes around seven hours. The nearest airport is 85 kilometres away in Kristiansand; from there you can reach the restaurant by car in around 1.5 hours. | **Hours** Evenings only; tables must be reserved online: www.under.no | **Tip** A few kilometres from the restaurant, on the southernmost tip of Norway, stands Lyndesnes Fyr, the country's oldest lighthouse.

53__Keukenhof

The largest flower garden

Keukenhof is one of the most photographed places in the Netherlands – and not only since the emergence of Instagram. This is understandable, as wherever you look you see flowers in the most brilliant colours. Every spring, Keukenhof opens its gates for eight weeks. Millions of flower heads then cover large sections of the 32-hectare park.

Back in the 15th century the grounds belonged to a Dutch countess. It was called 'Kuikenduin' – 'kitchen dune' – at the time, because the herbs for the countess' kitchen were grown here. Later a castle was built on the estate, and the garden became a large park complex in the English style – until a couple of Dutch bulb growers had the idea of using the place for an exhibition. In 1950, they presented their prettiest early-blossoming plants to the public at this location for the first time. Since then, the annual show has developed into one of the biggest tourist attractions in the Netherlands.

More than seven million flower bulbs are planted between old trees, pavilions and small watercourses here every year. Countless daffodils, hyacinths, crocuses and irises form creative patterns. But centre stage is the tulip, which blossoms in every imaginable variety of colour and form in Keukenhof. It is seen as *the* flower of Holland per se, but it actually originated in Asia Minor. The flowers came from the court of the Turkish sultan in the 16th century, via some detours, into the Netherlands, where a form of tulip mania broke out. At one point, the price of bulbs even exceeded that of gold many times over.

Today there is no other place in the world where you can experience such a striking diversity of tulip blossoms as at Keukenhof. The floral splendour is fleeting, however: in the middle of May the blossoms begin to wilt and the park closes. But the beauty of the flowers is preserved thanks to the myriad of photographs taken by visitors.

Address Stationsweg 166A, 2161 AM Lisse, The Netherlands | Getting there From
Schiphol airport there is an express bus directly to Keukenhof (around 30 minutes). | Hours
Mid-Mar to mid-May daily 8am – 7.30pm | Tip Between Amsterdam and Lisse is the Royal
Flora Holland, the largest flower auction hall in the world. Every day around 40 million
flowers are auctioned and sold. Visitors can also watch the auctions, Mon – Fri from 7am.

54__ The Curonian Spit
The longest beach

There are few places in Europe where you can still go for long, solitary walks on the beach. Too many people crowd on to the Adriatic coast and the Algarve, Costa Brava and Côte d'Azur – especially in peak season. But there is a stretch of coast on which you have the chance, even in summer, to stroll along the sand for hours on end and hardly see a soul: the Curonian Spit. For one, this corner of Europe is far from being as overrun by tourism as other regions; for another, there is a lot of space: the beach on the narrow Baltic Sea peninsula is 98 kilometres long.

Russia and Lithuania share the headland, which is completely made up of sand and shifting dunes. It separates the Curonian Lagoon from the Baltic Sea. The spit measures almost 4,000 metres at its widest point, but not even 400 metres at the narrowest. You can hear the rumble of waves from almost anywhere. From the crests of the metre-high dunes the view stretches to the glittering water of the lagoon on one side, and to the churning Baltic Sea surf on the other. It apparently made such an impression on the novelist Thomas Mann that he built himself a summer house here.

The Curonian Spit was created during the last Ice Age. Where huge sand dunes dominate the picture today, there once stood thick forest. But with the wood used for shipbuilding and other purposes, the primeval forest was cleared, which meant that the sand was able to pile up. This resulted in the creation of huge, shifting dunes, and the complete burying of whole villages, at the mercy of the wind and sand.

From the 1870s the spit was intensively planted and reforested again in order to stabilise it, as a result of which the dunes stopped shifting. Today the entire Curonian Spit is a protected nature reserve. If you visit the 'Sahara of the north', you are sure to find one thing above all: peace and pure nature.

Getting there From the Lithuanian side you can only reach the spit by ferry from Klaipėda. From the Russian side, public buses travel daily from Kaliningrad to the Curonian Spit. You'll need a visa to cross the border between the Lithuanian and Russian areas. | **Tip** Take a trip on a traditional Kurenkahn on the lagoon. These wooden sailing boats were historically used for transportation and fishing.

55_Unstad

The most northerly surfers' paradise

When Thor Frantzen and Hans Egil Krane undertook the first attempts to ride the waves in Unstad at the start of the 1960s, they had neither surfboard nor thick neoprene suits. They had both worked previously as skippers on cargo ships, which had taken them to Australia. They marvelled at the surfers on the famous Bondi Beach, and returned to their homeland of Norway completely impassioned. There were waves there too, after all! As a result they built themselves their own boards out of polystyrene sourced from old fish boxes. Then they wrapped themselves up in thick woollen jumpers and waterproof raincoats to protect against the cold, and plunged into the icy North Sea.

Today, surfers are no longer a rare sight in the tiny town on the Norwegian Lofoten island of Vestvågøy – although these days they wear much more familiar kit. Here, more than 150 kilometres north of the Arctic Circle, a real surfers' Mecca has developed. The best conditions prevail in the small bay off Unstad, surrounded by high rock faces. The waves here are usually not huge, but on many days they are perfectly formed for surfing.

Now word has spread, and an increasing number of surfers from all over the world visit Unstad in order to test their limits. Surfing here certainly isn't a sport for the faint-hearted. Even in summer the sea remains dreadfully cold, and in winter the water temperatures are in single digits. Snow can fall even in spring or autumn. It's not rare to surf here with a view of white mountains and a snow-covered beach. With a bit of luck surfers can even see the northern lights while gliding over the waves.

In the meantime, there's not only a surf shop in Unstad, but also a surf camp, where even beginners venture into the icy tides. There is at least one thing you don't have to worry about here: unlike Australia and Hawaii, there are no dangerous sharks in Norway.

Address Unstadveien, 8360 Unstad, Lofoten, Norway | Getting there By air via Oslo to Leknes on Vestvågøy, then around 20 kilometres by rental car | Tip The best time for beginners is May to September; in winter the swell is higher, and only suitable for experienced surfers.

56 British Library

The library with the most items

The British Library was once described in parliament as 'one of the ugliest buildings in the world'. The new building near London's St Pancras Station was not exactly showered with love when it opened in 1997. Many remembered the famous domed reading room in the British Museum, where most of the library's books were previously housed, with melancholy. Karl Marx had written parts of *Capital* there, and famous writers such as Charles Dickens, George Bernard Shaw and Virginia Woolf were regular guests.

But the museum was beginning to bulge at the seams. In 1973, the British Museum Library and some other institutions were brought together as the new National Library. Not only books and magazines, but also audio recordings, maps, databases, paintings, stamps and patents are part of the collection. There are more than 170 million items in total, with around 8,000 new ones added every day. In order to create room for the immense deluge of media, the building in St Pancras, which is now the library's main site, was built.

True treasures of the history of humankind are stored behind the walls of the modern building. The oldest objects in the collection come from the period around 1,600 years before Christ. Among the most precious are two original Magna Cartas and two Gutenberg Bibles. The British Library also calls the oldest completely preserved book in Europe its own: a transcript of the Gospel of John from the early 8th century. The catalogue includes works from almost every period, country and language. Many are extremely valuable, like the copies of the first complete works of Shakespeare or the diaries of Leonardo da Vinci.

The inventory of the British Library is absolutely unique. And even the unpopular new build has redeemed itself in the meantime. In 2015, a preservation order was put on it – as one of the youngest buildings ever.

Address 96 Euston Road, London NW1 2DB, England | **Getting there** Underground to King's Cross St Pancras, Euston or Euston Square | **Hours** Mon–Thu 9.30am–8pm, Fri 9.30am–6pm, Sat 9.30am–5pm, Sun 11am–5pm; information on opening times of individual reading rooms at: www.bl.uk | **Tip** The British Library also makes part of its holdings available online. Access around four million works via the website.

57___London Eye
The tallest Ferris wheel

The London Eye is the perfect refuge in the middle of the British capital. On the streets of the metropolis, with its population of nine million, endless streams of pedestrians push past each other, with everyone seemingly in a hurry. But you can leave all the noise, cars and people behind – or more specifically below you – sealed off from the hustle and bustle in one of the big wheel's 32 gondolas.

The 135-metre wheel turns slowly, right on the banks of the Thames, opposite the majestic Big Ben and Westminster Palace. Created on the occasion of the new millennium, the design of the wheel represents a distinct contrast to the Victorian architecture that characterises so much of the centre of the British capital. 1,700 tonnes of steel were used in its construction, which from a distance looks like an oversized bicycle wheel. The gondolas are attached to the outside to ensure that nothing obscures the passengers' view as they look out from the fully-glazed capsules. There is room for a total of up to 800 visitors at a time to travel in the London Eye's elliptical gondolas.

The big wheel turns so slowly that you hardly notice that you're moving away from the ground. At first you see only the glittering water of the Thames, then you are suddenly at eye level with some of the most important sights of the city. Westminster Abbey and Big Ben seem close enough to touch, then a little further on is Buckingham Palace. Looking towards the north east, the Tower of London and St Paul's Cathedral come into view. In good weather it's possible to see for up to 40 kilometres – and if you're lucky, perhaps even make out Windsor Castle.

The city sightseeing tour from a bird's-eye view takes around half an hour. Then the time out from the turmoil of London ends, and out of the glass capsule you step, back into the crowds and hubbub of the British capital.

Address Westminster Bridge Road, London SE1 7PB, England | Getting there Underground to Waterloo, Embankment, Charing Cross or Westminster | Hours Mon–Fri 11am–6pm, Sat & Sun 10am–8.30pm | Tip The architects of the London Eye have also designed a modern viewing tower for Brighton in the south of England. A glazed viewing pulpit travels to a height of up to 138 metres, from which you can enjoy views of the beach, town and surrounding area.

58 Malbork Castle

The largest brick castle

It looks like a knight's castle from a book of traditional fairy tales: Malbork Castle, in the Polish town of the same name. Thick walls with battlements and defence towers surround the complex, with impressive castle buildings and church walls looming up behind them. You almost expect a knight on horseback with a shield and lance to gallop cross the bridge over the Nogat river in front of the magnificent structure.

Malbork Castle, around 60 kilometres south-east of Danzig, is an impressive legacy of the Middle Ages, and represents a piece of German-Polish history. It was German Teutonic Knights who built the castle. During the period of the crusades the knights of the order had helped in the missionary work of the Christian Church. They had ridden through Eastern Europe to the Holy Land, and established branches in many places. Malbork was created from 1270 as an important base. In 1309 the Grandmaster of the German Order relocated his seat here, which increased the importance of the castle even more. The fortress was upgraded to a castle – composed of many millions of red bricks, giving the castle its characteristic appearance to this day, and making it the largest brick building in Europe.

Malbork Castle, or Marienburg as it was at the time, was in the hands of the German Order until 1457. Then the fortress fell to Poland. The following centuries were eventful, and characterised by many battles. The complex suffered its heaviest blow during World War II, when large parts of the fortress were destroyed. It is thanks to the comprehensive Polish reconstruction that took place in the 1960s and 1970s that the castle can now be viewed again in its original appearance, as the famous site was immaculately restored. It has been a UNESCO World Heritage Site since 1997 – and is one of the country's most significant historical sights.

Address Starościńska 1, 82–200 Malbork, Poland | **Getting there** From Danzig reach Malbork by regional train in around half an hour; from the railway station walk for around 15 minutes | **Hours** Daily May–Sept 9am–8pm, Oct–Apr 10am–4pm | **Tip** Every year in July the siege of Malbork Castle by the Polish-Lithuanian army in 1410 is re-enacted as a grand open-air spectacle. A medieval market and archery tournament accompany the event.

59__Stara Trta

The oldest living vine

A copperplate in the 'Old Vine House' museum shows a view of the city of Maribor from the year 1657. The Stara Trta, the oldest vine in Europe, is apparently depicted in it, as a green detail on the facade of a medieval house that was once part of the city walls. The vine of the Žametovka grape variety continues to climb along precisely this house wall in the Lent neighbourhood on the left bank of the Drava to this day. It is more than 400 years old, and still bears fruit every year.

There is a tradition of wine growing in Maribor, the hilly vineyards reach all the way up to the edges of the Slovenian city. There were times in which it was the dry white wines of the region that were particularly well known beyond the country's borders. That the Stara Trta in Maribor has been able to assert itself over the centuries is a small miracle. It not only survived the vine pest, which destroyed many European vines in the 19th century, but also survived fires, sieges and bombings unharmed – partly thanks to the robust variety of the vine. In 1972, experts proved that it is indeed a Methuselah among vines on the basis of samples taken from the trunk: under an electron microscope they counted more than 350 growth rings.

Today the plant thrives between two younger offshoot vines, and produces around 50 kilograms of grapes every year, with around 30 litres of wine made from these grapes. The sweet red wine is not the finest of drops, but unique due to its history. It is presented to prominent guests of state in specially designed bottles. During the annual cutting of the vine, scions are also given to partner cities. In the meantime, there are descendants of the Stara Trta growing in more than 160 locations around the world, including Paris, the Vatican and Prague. In this way, the continued existence of the oldest vine in Europe is secured.

Address Vojašniška ulica 8, 2000 Maribor, Slovenia | Getting there The train from Ljubljana to Maribor takes around 2.5 hours, then it's a 15-minute walk to Stara Trta. | Tip Every autumn Maribor celebrates the 'Old Vine Festival' on the occasion of the grape harvest of the Stara Trta, with wine tasting and numerous Slovenian culinary specialities.

60__ Staatliche Porzellan-Manufaktur Meissen

The oldest porcelain factory

You certainly need a steady hand to be a porcelain painter. Particularly if you want to decorate a piece with the most successful of all patterns: the onion pattern. In delicate strokes of blue on a white background, to this day it continues to be painted by hand in Meissen. After all, the small Saxon city is not only the birthplace of the famous motif, but of European porcelain.

In 1710, Augustus II the Strong, Elector of Saxony, announced the establishment of a porcelain factory. The production site in the Albrechtsburg in Meissen became the first of its kind in Europe. Until then, the material was only known as coming from China, where porcelain had already been used for many centuries. It wasn't until the start of the 18th century, however, that the alchemist Johann Friedrich Böttger was able to decipher the secret of its production. His recipe for the mixture of white kaolin, feldspar and quartz formed the foundation for the international success of the factory.

Around 700,000 model forms have been made in the course of the company's more than 300-year history. Some are still used for production today. Every piece is still formed, fired and glazed by hand in a painstaking process. The paints for the elaborate porcelain painting are manufactured in the in-house laboratory according to old formulations, such as the cobalt blue used for the renowned onion pattern.

Very few people know that the onions weren't originally onions at all. In fact, this pattern had also been copied from China. The motifs depicted there were peaches, pomegranates and citrons – exotic fruit unfamiliar to the Saxon painters. As a result, their stylised depictions looked more like onions. In retrospect, this probably represents one of the most successful misinterpretations in history.

Address Talstraße 9, 01662 Meissen, Germany | **Getting there** From Dresden you reach Meissen via the S-train line 1 in half an hour. From Meissen-Triebischtal walk around 500 metres. | **Hours** Daily 9am–5pm | **Tip** During the guided tours you can watch how the porcelain is painted in the show workshops. Now and then creative workshops are also on offer, where visitors can learn the basics of the craft.

61__Circuit de Monaco
The only Formula 1 city circuit

It is the slowest race in the Formula 1 calendar – yet anything but boring. On the contrary: Circuit de Monaco is considered one of the most spectacular and demanding tracks in the series. This is because it leads right through the densely built city state of Monaco, which is known especially for its concentration of millionaires.

A Formula 1 Grand Prix took place on the Côte d'Azur for the first time in 1950. From today's perspective, the course is the exact opposite of modern racing tracks, in which safety comes first. In 78 laps, each exactly 3.337 kilometres long, the cars race through the narrow alleyways of the mundane Monte Carlo and La Condamine neighbourhoods, often scraping past some of the world's most expensive real estate.

The incredibly powerful machines make 11 right-hand turns and eight left turns as they snake through the city. And while the Monégasques drive at speeds of up to 50 kilometres an hour, the racing drivers can reach 290! Overtaking on the narrow streets is almost impossible. On no other course are so many demands made of the drivers, and their skill so tested – and nowhere else do small mistakes immediately have such high cost. This is why a victory in Monaco is considered a special feat among the drivers – and for many fans, the race is a highlight of each F1 season.

Not only the race course, but also the backdrop of the event is special in the small principality. The Monaco Grand Prix is by far the most dazzling event in Formula 1. Yachts costing millions are moored in the harbour in front of the paddock, the quay becomes a catwalk for stars and wannabes. The racing is almost incidental by the time evening comes, when parties break out in all the bars and restaurants. Formula 1 in Monaco is a cocktail of adrenalin and glamour. A mixture that makes the Circuit de Monaco unique for both Formula 1 drivers and fans alike.

Address Boulevard Albert 1er, 98000 Monaco | **Getting there** The race track is only a few minutes' walk from Monaco-Monte-Carlo railway station. The Monaco Grand Prix takes place every year in May. | **Tip** Spend an evening in the legendary Monte Carlo Casino, which has served as the backdrop for the James Bond classics *Never Say Never Again* and *GoldenEye*.

62 Ostankino Tower
The tallest television tower

There really isn't a lack of impressive sights in Moscow – especially not in the area around Red Square. The most popular attractions are concentrated in the smallest of spaces in the heart of the Russian capital. Between the colourful onion domes of Saint Basil's Cathedral, the famous department store GUM, Lenin's Mausoleum and the red Kremlin walls, masses of visitors compete with one another in the modern sport of selfie-taking.

A little way away from the hustle and bustle, in the north of the million-citizen metropolis, another eye-catching edifice shoots solitarily up from the ground: the television tower Ostankino, named after the neighbourhood it is surrounded by. Embedded in the grounds of the 'Exhibition of Achievements of National Economy' it seems like a flagship project of the former Soviet Union. It reaches up to the sky like a rocket about to lift-off, a slim shaft on a conical foot, on the top a steel mast as antenna carrier. The construction of steel and concrete is 540 metres tall. After its opening in 1967, the Ostankino was even the tallest free-standing building in the world. More than 50 years later it is still the tallest building, and thus also the tallest television tower, in Europe.

19 television channels and more than a dozen radio signals are broadcast from here. Those who wish to visit the tower must therefore stick to strict safety regulations. Three high-speed lifts bring visitors to the viewing platform, which is at an altitude of 337 metres. When the weather is good you can see large parts of the mega city from up here.

Below the platform is the Seventh Heaven restaurant. Thanks to the turning floor, you have a 360-degree panoramic view of the Russian capital while drinking your coffee. You can also see Red Square, with its distinctive buildings from the television tower – but from a very new perspective.

Address Akademika Koroleva Street 15, 127427 Moscow, Russia | **Getting there** Metro line 6 to WDNCh, then trolleybus (line 36 or 73) to Ulitca Akademika Korolyova, or by monorail (line 13) to Telezentr | **Hours** Daily 10am–11pm | **Tip** In the 'Exhibition of Achievements of National Economy' park, gain insight into the idealised self-portrayal of the former USSR. The exhibition ground was created in 1923, and is a protected historical site. Around 100 pavilions present flagship projects of the former republics of the Soviet Union.

63___LeapRus 3912
The highest altitude hotel

Mount Elbrus belongs to the 'Seven Summits' that are on the bucket list of many mountaineers. The massif is located in the south of Russia, in the middle of the Caucasus Mountains on the border of Europe and Asia. It is an inhospitable area with many rugged peaks, but above them all towers Mount Elbrus, with its highest peak 5,642 metres above sea level. This makes it – even ahead of Mont Blanc – the highest mountain on the European continent.

Those who wish to scale it can get to almost 3,850 metres by funicular, but from there the only way is on foot. Most mountaineers bring equipment with them and spend the night in tents or simple mountain huts – often without electricity or water. But since 2013, a three-star hotel has offered refuge to potential summit conquerors. The striking building comprises three white, tubular structures. Inside are the bedrooms and a restaurant, while the sanitary facilities are located in an outbuilding.

The accommodation is called LeapRus 3912, because it is located at an altitude of exactly 3,912 metres. To build at this lofty altitude was a logistical and design challenge for the architects. Individual parts of the hotel were prefabricated like a puzzle, and lifted on to the mountain by helicopter, where they were assembled in situ. This meant that the building materials had to be extremely light. The architects had to get creative in other parts of the design too. The water for washing and cooking, for example, is obtained from melted snow.

Admittedly, great luxury cannot be expected here. Guests sleep in a 12-bed room, and visiting the bathroom requires a walk through the bitter cold of the Caucasus! However, the hotel offers a little comfort in the harsh, mountainous environment, and one other thing visitors particularly appreciate: a perfect view of the summit of Mount Elbrus from the panoramic windows.

Address 361605 Terskol, Kabardino-Balkaria Republic, Russia | **Getting there** By air or train to Mineralnye Vody, then by shuttle or taxi to Terskol. From the valley station Poljana Asau take the funicular to Gara-Baschi at around 3,850 metres. From there, the hotel organises pick-up by snowcat. | **Hours** May – Sept | **Tip** For the ascent to the summit prior experience is essential, and in particular make sure to allow enough time to become acclimatised to the thin mountain air.

64_ Oktoberfest
The biggest fair

When Munich's mayor taps the first barrel of beer and exclaims 'O'zapft is!' at 12 on the dot, he is signalling the start of a fair of superlatives. More than six million visitors come to Oktoberfest on the Munich Theresienwiese every year. The partying, dancing, eating and drinking goes on for two weeks. It all starts to add up: more than seven million mugs of beer, almost 250,000 pairs of pork sausages and, believe it or not, half a million fried chicken meals are passed over the bars of the large beer tents. On top of that there's around 120 roast oxen, three dozen calves and almost 80,000 knuckles of pork. Then, of course, countless pretzels and gingerbread hearts.

But Oktoberfest is also about traditions. It began with a party on the occasion of the marriage of Ludwig I of Bavaria and Princess Therese of Saxe-Hildburghausen in 1810. A party was hosted for the people, and was so popular that it went on to be celebrated annually. Over the years more and more showmen and funfair rides have been included, with the Munich breweries erecting large tents, in which they served beer and provided entertainment with brass bands. Right up into the 19th century some innkeepers would drive to their tents with magnificently decorated horses and carts. This became the 'Entry of the Innkeepers', and is now one of the highlights of Oktoberfest. The ceremonial tapping of the first barrel has been a fixed part of the programme since 1950. And the classic costumes – dirndl and lederhosen – are *the* dress code on the so-called Wiesn, not only among Bavarian visitors.

Old customs and well-preserved traditions, packaged in a well-oiled, modern entertainment machine – that is the Oktoberfest recipe for success. This recipe has also been exported in the meantime, with spin-offs of the largest European fair taking place around the world, from Brazil to China to the West Bank.

Address Theresienwiese, Bavariaring, 80336 Munich, Germany | Getting there By underground (U 4 or U 5) to Theresienwiese, alternatively U 3 or U 6 to Goetheplatz or Poccistraße | Hours Oktoberfest begins on the Saturday after September 15 and lasts two weeks, with beer tents open Mon – Fri 10am – 11.30pm, Sat & Sun 9am – 11.30pm | Tip If you want to take things easy, visit the 'Oide Wiesn' in the southern part of the site: here things are a lot more sedate – with historical rides, classic brass bands and nostalgic stalls.

65__Praia do Norte
The biggest surfing waves

Nazaré's fame began in 2011. Before then hardly anyone knew about the small fishing village on the Portuguese Atlantic coast. Certainly not in the surfer scene. But the former mayor recognised the potential of the enormous waves that unfurl their power every winter off the coast of Nazaré. As a result, he brought one of the best big-wave surfers in the world to Portugal – and made the place famous in a single stroke.

It was Garrett McNamara who put Nazaré on the international surfing map. The US-American actually lives in Hawaii, the Mecca of big-wave surfing. After the mayor of Nazaré invited him to the village, he conquered an almost 24-metre monster wave in November 2011, and in doing so found himself in the *Guinness Book of Records*. The 'largest ever surfed wave in the world' at the time made international headlines. Since then, professional surfers from all around the world have been drawn to the small town around 120 kilometres north of Lisbon, trying to trump each other in riding the huge waves. Tourists visit in hoards to watch the dangerous spectacle from the beach.

The waves off Nazaré grow to the size of skyscrapers, especially in winter, when storms rage on the Atlantic. This is due to a deep underwater trench that abruptly narrows around 300 metres off the shore. The sea floor rises up like a step, and forces the enormous masses of water upwards. This is what creates the giant waves, which can reach over 30 metres in height, and race towards the coast with enormous speed. Surfing in these conditions is extremely dangerous. A surfer who falls can be overwhelmed by hundreds of tonnes of water, and pressed beneath the surface, sometimes for minutes. But that doesn't daunt passionate surfers such as McNamara, who has been returning to Nazaré time and again ever since that first visit – always in the hope of riding an even bigger wave.

Address Praia do Norte, 2450–065 Nazaré, Portugal | **Getting there** It is less than a two-hour drive from Lisbon to Nazaré, with Praia do Norte on the northern edge of town. | **Tip** If you're hungry, visit the A Celeste restaurant on the beach promenade: this fish restaurant is Garrett McNamara's regular haunt. The owners even have a menu with his favourite dishes on offer.

66 Northern Ireland
The most Game of Thrones *filming locations*

Rugged coasts, historic castles and enchanted forests – it comes as no surprise that the location scouts for *Game of Thrones* found a variety of settings for their fantasy saga in Northern Ireland. More than 30 places here served as backdrops for the successful fantasy series – more than in any other country. Most of these locations can be accessed by visitors, and are now pilgrimage sites for hardcore *Game of Thrones* fans from around the world.

One example is Ward Castle in County Down, south-east of Belfast. The medieval manor house was already transformed into the Winterfell fortress for the pilot episode. As the family seat of the Starks, the property became a central location in the series. Visitors can now emulate the characters of the series in the castle's courtyard, and try their hand at archery or axe throwing – all while wearing authentic costume, of course.

Not far away is another famous setting: the old trees and Gothic stone arches of Tollymore Forest. These offered the perfect backdrop for the cursed forest, in which the guards of the Night's Watch encounter the White Walkers. The famous scene in which Ned Stark discovers the direwolves with his sons was also shot here by a stream. Another highlight for every fan is the Dark Hedges of Ballymoney, right in the north of the country. The picturesque avenue, lined by crooked beech trees, became the Kingsroad, which Arya Stark used to flee north dressed as a boy in the second season. The location only featured briefly in the series, but that was enough to make the beech avenue one of the most photographed sights of the country. With its chequered political history, Northern Ireland has long stood in the shadow of its bigger brother to the south in terms of tourism, but the success of *Game of Thrones* and the accessibility of locations from the saga has given the region an enormous boost.

Getting there All locations can be reached by car in less than two hours from Belfast. You can explore them under your own steam, or from the capital join a guided *Game of Thrones* tour. | Tip If you want to check out the filming locations without a guide, the official *Game of Thrones* app from Northern Ireland Screen will help. All of the locations open to the public are marked on a map, plus information about their 'appearances' in the series.

67___Kusttram

The longest tram route

Children in swimming trunks, families packed like donkeys laden with cool boxes and parasols, and even sporty types with surfboards – they all squeeze into the carriages of the Kusttram. The summer months are peak season for the longest tram line in Europe. In around two and a half hours, it travels the whole length of the coast of Belgium, from Knokke-Heist in the north-east of the country, just over the border from Holland, to De Panne in the south-west, where you are almost in France.

The tram makes 67 stops along the Belgian North Sea coast, on a route that is 67 kilometres long. The narrow-gauge railway rattles at a relaxed pace through chic seaside resorts, which alternate with dreary industrial areas and plain apartment complexes. Now and then the view opens up to reveal gentle dunes, small forests and the green-blue expanse of the North Sea.

The first section of the route was opened way back in 1885. During the Belle Époque, the wealthy bourgeoisie in particular recuperated on the Belgian coast. Seaside resorts along the tram route, such as De Haan, bear witness to this period to this day. Here, even the historic station building is still preserved, with many of the old villas having been lovingly restored.

Further south, passengers can reach Oostende, where Karl Marx and Friedrich Engels enjoyed the summer freshness. The most pleasant section of the route begins just beyond Oostende, where the Kusttram hugs the sea shore. Only a narrow path separates the tracks from the sand, and the waves seem to be within touching distance. The beach grows ever wider towards France, while in Oostduinkerke it's possible to see the last crabbers, who hunt with trawling nets on the beach by horse – a unique custom. At this point it is only a few kilometres to De Panne – the most westerly point of Belgium, and the terminus of the longest tram line in Europe.

Address The Kusttram plies between Knokke-Heist and De Panne | **Getting there** Both Knokke and De Panne are easy to reach by train from the Belgian capital, Brussels. | **Hours** Information on timetables is available at: www.delijn.be | **Tip** Every three years, installations by artists from around the world are created along the entire coast of Belgium during the Beaufort Festival. Many works of art are now permanently installed, and turn the coastal strip into a large open-air gallery.

68_Passion Play
The largest amateur theatre

In real life they are press officers, hoteliers, pupils or wood sculptors – but in Oberammergau they become the stars of a unique theatre production. Every 10 years the inhabitants of the small Bavarian town perform the Passion Play – amateur dramatics on a gigantic scale. Around 2,000 Oberammergau residents – almost half of the town's population – stand together on the stage to present the story of the Passion of Christ.

This is a unique tradition with a long history. During the Thirty Years' War, the plague spread rampantly throughout Europe. Oberammergau was no exception, and the Black Death took more than 80 lives in the village. In order to ward off the wrath of God, the residents vowed to perform the Passion Play every 10 years from then on. The people of Oberammergau have stayed true to their word, and for almost 400 years have brought the 5-hour production to the stage once a decade.

The preparations begin almost a year in advance, when actors are cast in their roles. Only those born in Oberammergau or who have lived there for at least 20 years can take part. From toddlers to great grandmothers, members of every generation have roles in the production, even though a part in the Passion Play demands quite a lot from them. Many have to fit their work around the schedule during rehearsals, or even take time off work for a period now and then. Then there's the 'hair and beard decree': beginning on Ash Wednesday, all of the actors have to let their hair grow – and the men their beards too – so they visually embody the roles they are to play as well as possible.

The production is performed five days a week for five months, in front of almost half a million viewers from all over the world. It is a feat of strength – for the actors and the whole village – but also a demonstration of what community and togetherness can achieve.

Address Passionswiese 1, 82487 Oberammergau, Germany | Getting there From Munich by regional train via Murnau to Oberammergau | Hours Every 10 years, more than 100 performances May–Oct, except Mon and Wed; more information available from www.passionsspiele-oberammergau.de | Tip Reserve tickets well in advance: although around half a million are available, the performances are often sold out months ahead.

69__ The Literary Man
The hotel with the biggest library

For many, a holiday is the perfect time to read. You can finally find the peace and quiet necessary to lose yourself in a good book. But when you check in to The Literary Man hotel in the small Portuguese city of Óbidos, you could quickly find yourself overwhelmed. Here, a huge library awaits holidaying bookworms: there are a total of 65,000 titles to choose from – many more than even the most enthusiastic reader could manage in a lifetime, let alone a holiday!

The hotel is housed in the old walls of a former monastery, only a few minutes' walk from the famous medieval castle of Óbidos. Since 2015 it has been all about books – and they are ever-present: you'll find them in the dining room, in the bedrooms and corridors, even in the hotel bar.

From thrillers and bestsellers to coffee-table books, from children's books to historical works and specialist literature – every genre and subject you could imagine is represented. Most of the editions are in English, but The Literary Man also has Portuguese, French and German titles on offer. Those who want to read a book can simply take it to their room, or make themselves comfortable on the sofa in front of the hotel's fireplace.

For some years Óbidos has tried to establish itself as a 'literary city'. As a result, you'll find books in unusual places when strolling through the historic alleyways. For example, there are books in a church from the 12th century, which has been repurposed as a library and bookshop, and also at the organic market, where books in fruit baskets are for sale alongside cabbages and oranges.

The Literary Man hotel fits well into this concept with its library. Guests who want to take books home with them at the end of their stay can buy them, but in truth, it's often the other way around: many guests donate books they brought with them, and in doing so contribute to expanding the hotel's literary collection.

Address Rua Dom João D'Ornelas, 2510–074 Óbidos, Portugal | Getting there Óbidos is around 85 kilometres from Lisbon, and can be reached in around 2.5 hours by train; from the station it's a 15-minute walk to the hotel. | Tip In the hotel bar you can also enjoy a very literary end to the evening, sipping cocktails inspired by famous authors or books.

70__Westray–Papa Westray

The shortest scheduled flight

It will probably take longer to read this chapter of this book than it takes for the small propeller plane to make the flight from Westray to Papa Westray. That's how close the two islands of the Orkney archipelago off the north coast of Scotland are to one another. However, there's no bridge between them, and ferry connections are both unreliable and quite time-consuming. That's why the Scottish airline Loganair offers a regular flight connection between the islands on an almost daily basis.

The runways at large international airports such as London Heathrow are longer than the whole route here, with only 2.7 kilometres separating the take-off and landing sites. The scheduled flight time for this short journey? Just 90 seconds – even less if there's a tailwind! The record time for the ultra-short-haul flight is a mere 47 seconds. Up to eight passengers can travel in the twin-engine aircraft, and the ones sitting right at the front can comfortably watch over the pilot's shoulder and enjoy the view from the cockpit – although not for very long!

Almost 600 people live on Westray, and not even 100 on Papa Westray, but the flight connection between them represents an important lifeline for the residents of these Scottish islands. Many people use the airline service to get to work or school, for example, and the scheduled flight is also essential for medical care. For this reason, the Scottish government subsidises the flights, thereby making prices affordable.

Soon, the shortest scheduled flight in Europe could attract attention for another reason: it's set to become the first electric scheduled flight on the continent, as the airline plans to convert its planes into e-aircraft. The short route between Westray and Papa Westray would definitely be the ideal location to test battery-powered flight – at least there would certainly be no need for range anxiety!

Address Westray Airport, 1 Sand o'Gill, Westray, KW17 2DN, Orkney Islands, Scotland | **Getting there** Starting point for visits is Kirkwall in the Orkneys, from which you reach the islands of Westray or Papa Westray by ferry or plane. | **Hours** Connections from Papa Westray to Westray daily except Sat, in the other direction daily except Sun; more info at: www.loganair.co.uk | **Tip** Knap of Howar on Papa Westray is worth a visit – the two buildings are from the Neolithic period, and are more than 5,000 years old.

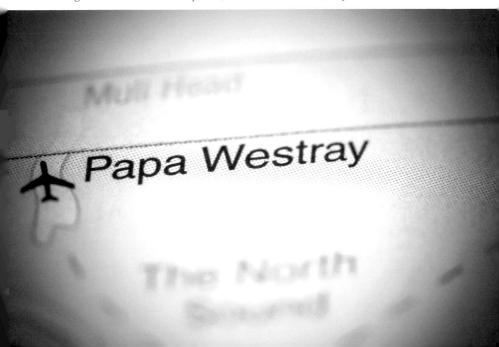

71__Orto Botanico di Padova
The oldest botanical garden

One of the biggest treasures of Padua's botanical garden is hidden behind the glass shell of a small, octagonal greenhouse: *Chamaerops humilis*, a dwarf palm, which has stood here for almost 450 years. Several trunks grow close together, directed towards the sky, where the impressive, fan-shaped leaves of the palm form a thick, green canopy. It is the oldest plant in the garden – and also has the most prominent history. Johann Wolfgang von Goethe once saw exactly this specimen. When the German poet visited the Italian city in the year 1786, the palm is thought to have inspired his text *Metamorphosis of Plants*. That the tree has now outlived its most famous visitor by almost two centuries is quite remarkable.

The 'Goethe Palm' is only one of around 3,500 species that are currently on show in the botanical garden. Orto Botanico di Padova was established in 1545 as the medicinal garden of the University of Padua. The students were to research the healing powers of plants, and at the same time learn to distinguish the benign from the poisonous specimens. After all, herbal remedies represented an important form of medical care at the time. Over the course of hundreds of years, exotic plants also joined the medicinal plants on the site, and the botanical garden became a place of biodiversity. Today, it houses flora from every possible region and climate zone in the world.

As the oldest institution of its kind, 1997 saw the facility recognised as a World Heritage Site by UNESCO. But the fact that it is old doesn't mean it is old-fashioned. For some time now it's been possible for visitors to obtain information about individual stations and plants on a visit to the botanical garden via an app. And perhaps through this they come to share the conclusion that Goethe himself reached: 'Be in awe of plants, as everything lives through them.'

Address Via Orto Botanico 15, 35123 Padua, Italy | **Getting there** Around 25 minutes by train from Venice to Padua, then reach the botanical garden by tram (Santo) | **Hours** Daily 9am–7pm (Apr/May), Tue–Sun 9am–7pm (June–Sept), 9am–6pm (Oct), 9am–5pm (Nov–Mar) | **Tip** Right next to the university and the botanical garden is the impressive Prato della Valle, a 90,000-square-metre plaza with 78 statues, and the imposing Abbey of Santa Giustina.

72_Le Grand Rex
The largest cinema auditorium

It was a cold December day in 1932 that saw more than 3,000 Parisians flock to Boulevard Poissonnière in the second Arrondissement, the men dressed in elegant suits, the women in sequinned evening dresses. It was the opening night of the Le Grand Rex. 80 members of staff in tailcoats and white gloves led the guests inside, where many of them could not believe their eyes.

For the film producer Jacques Haïk, this was a childhood dream being fulfilled. He had the cinema built in the style of the grand American film palaces. With its distinctive Art Deco facade and the huge name sign, it was already an eye-catching sight from the outside. But from the very beginning the huge cinema auditorium, with its 3,300 seats, was the main attraction. Like in a theatre, the room is divided into three tiers: parterre, mezzanine and circle. Italian balconies, Greco-Roman statues and elaborate decorations characterise the extravagant decor. And above it all is a dark blue night sky with a myriad of stars – a tribute to the big movie legends, many of whom have visited Le Grand Rex over the years.

Even in the early period many premiere parties were held here, including Walter Lang's *The Little Princess*, featuring Shirley Temple in the lead role. Gary Cooper visited Paris in 1957 for the inauguration of the first ever cinema escalator, while Liz Taylor introduced *Cleopatra* here in 1963. Peter Jackson, Quentin Tarantino, Angelina Jolie, Martin Scorsese and Leonardo DiCaprio – the list of visitors reads like a *Who's Who* of the film industry.

It is the special atmosphere that attracts the stars to Le Grand Rex. Its ambience is reminiscent of the golden age of film – a time in which the cinema still possessed a touch of magic. This historic building has been listed since 1981, ensuring the nostalgic charm of the film palace will continue to be enjoyed by visitors for many years to come.

Address 1 Boulevard Poissonnière, 75002 Paris, France | **Getting there** Take Metro 8 or 9 to Bonne Nouvelle | **Hours** Viewings are possible with audio guide or on a guided tour: Wed, Sat & Sun, 10am – 6pm | **Tip** In the cellar of the cinema you can experience long party nights in the Rex Club. Originally opened as a chic dance café with live music, today the DJs mainly play electronic music.

73_Louvre
The most visited museum

She is the most sought-after woman in Paris: the *Mona Lisa*. Pretty much anyone who visits the French capital is familiar with this enigmatic subject of portraiture. Indeed, Leonardo da Vinci's masterpiece is the undisputed star of the Louvre's art collection, despite being surrounded by many other, equally impressive examples.

The museum houses more than half a million works of art. Around 38,000 of them are part of the exhibition. A turn through the Louvre is like a journey through time, visiting the milestones of the history of art. Paintings by the old masters such as Caravaggio, Tizian and Hieronymus Bosch are displayed in close proximity to sculptures like *Nike of Samothrake* and *Venus de Milo*. As well as paintings, drawings and graphics, jewellery and ceramics are also on show, with more than 400 rooms packed with the world's finest artistic works.

The Louvre was actually built as a royal palace. When Louis XIV – the 'Sun King' – moved to Versailles with his court in 1682, the city took over the building, and in the course of the French Revolution it became a museum. Today, art resides in the Parisian city palace, with the *Mona Lisa* as its queen. People travel from all over the world to see her. 2019 was a record-breaking year, seeing around 9.6 million visitors. A lot of patience is required when there's such a throng: visitors can wait for up to three hours in front of the Louvre's famous glass pyramid before being admitted to the museum.

Those who finally make it to exhibition hall number 711 – 'home' of the *Mona Lisa* – often catch only a fleeting glance of this surprisingly small painting at the end of the room. But fortunately, the mysterious beauty is not the only thing worth seeing in the Louvre, and once you've got your photo, you can enjoy the many other treasures on display in the most visited museum in Europe.

Address 99 Rue de Rivoli, 75001 Paris, France | Getting there Metro 1 or 7 to Palais-Royal Musée du Louvre | Hours Mon, Thu, Sat & Sun 9am–6pm, Wed & Fri 9am–9:45pm; on the first Saturday of the month admission is free 9am–9:45pm | Tip There are three different ways to get into the Louvre, with the entrances via Porte des Lions or Galerie du Carrousel usually less crowded than the main entrance by the glass pyramid.

74 Postojnska jama
The biggest stalactite cave

It's not especially pretty. With its pale, almost translucent skin, eel-like form and the red cluster of gills on the back of its head, the olm certainly isn't going to be winning any animal beauty contests. While it's only 30 centimetres long, this creature can live for up to a century, and is able to survive without food for years. To top it off, the olm doesn't see by using eyes, but rather through the use of its light-sensitive skin. This unusual creature is the most famous resident of the caves of Postojna. Indeed, the birth of an olm was captured on video for the first time here in the Slovenian province. As a result, many visitors hope for an encounter with the mysterious creature.

Around 24 kilometres of underground corridors form the gigantic cave system in the south-west of Slovenia, only part of which is accessible to visitors. The exploratory tour starts on a small electric train. Once they have progressed deep enough into the cave, visitors are required to continue on foot. Cavities open up, studded with numerous, fancifully formed dripstones that have developed at an imperceptible pace over the passing millennia. One of the most distinctive formations is called 'Brilliant': it is five metres tall and bright white. The droplets of water run persistently along the stone and accumulate a shiny calcite layer. A little further on, in the 'Red Hall', the stone is coloured red by iron oxide, while limestone dominates the 'White Hall'.

This is a diverse and fascinating world deep beneath the ground, but few visitors get to experience the olm – at least not in their natural habitat. While these shy animals do live in cave lakes, they do so much deeper in the ground. To enable tourists to see one, there's an aquarium in the cave, allowing observation of these strange creatures first-hand – and perhaps they'll even be able to witness the birth of a little olm.

Address Jamska cesta 30, 6230 Postojna, Slovenia | **Getting there** Buses from Ljubljana direct to the cave take around one hour, or take a train to Postojna then go on foot | **Hours** Daily from 9am, guided tours from May to Oct, hourly; out of season, three to four times a day | **Tip** Very nearby is Predjama Castle, the largest cave castle in the world, built in a recess on a rock face more than 120 metres tall.

76__Tromsø Golfklubb

The most northerly 18-hole golf course

As some locals joke, in Tromsø there are nine months of winter, and three months of bad conditions for skiing. This Norwegian city is around 350 kilometres north of the Arctic Circle. Between the end of November and the middle of January, during the polar night period, it is constantly dark, as the sun doesn't even rise. And as you might imagine, it is also cold, given the city's latitude. Even in the middle of summer it is rarely warm in Tromsø. So why should anyone want to visit a golf course in such an inhospitable environment?

The Tromsø Golfklubb was established in 1996. Located around 45 kilometres away from the city, it operates – against all odds – the most northerly 18-hole golf course in Europe. This is no easy task, as the lawns suffer considerable from the long cold season. The greenkeepers have their work cut out to offer a playable course to visitors. But the dreamlike surroundings compensate for the perhaps less than perfect greens. The sparsely populated region has its very own appeal. Here, golf is played against an impressive backdrop: the up to 1,800-metre-tall Lyngen Alps. You can almost see the nearby Ullsfjord when teeing off.

But because of the climatic conditions, the golf season of this city in the far north is extremely short. Fans of the sport are only able to get their fix between the end of May and the middle of October. However, in June and July they can also experience a highlight unavailable at any other golf course: during the polar days, when the sun is permanently in the sky, it's possible to swing your clubs at Tromsø around the clock! A round of golf in the light of the midnight sun – that is unique. It is the lust for light that is also celebrated in this way. For tourists it is a special experience during their holiday, while for the Norwegians, it represents welcome compensation following the long months of cold weather and daunting darkness.

Address Gnr 130 Bnr 11 Breivikeidet, 9027 Ramfjordbotn, Norway | Getting there Reach the golf course from Tromsø by car in around 45 minutes.| Hours End-May to mid-Oct; more information at www.tromsogolf.com | Tip A visit to the Arctic Cathedral in Tromsø is worthwhile. The interior of the distinctive church symbolises the long darkness and the northern lights. Its large glass mosaic window represents the midnight sun that breaks through the dark.

77___Charles Kuonen Bridge
The longest pedestrian suspension bridge

Fear of heights is certainly not the ideal condition for anyone proposing to walk over the suspension bridge near the small Swiss alpine village of Randa. It hangs 85 metres above the ground at the highest point, and through the gridded floor panels there's a constant clear view into the depths below – all the way along its record 494-metre length. Opened in 2017, this is the longest free-hanging pedestrian bridge in Europe.

The bridge traverses a gap in the Europaweg. The popular hiking route, located in the Swiss canton of Wallis, leads from the village of Grächen to Zermatt, at the foot of the famous Matterhorn. An earlier bridge that spanned the Matter valley near Randa, at a length of around 250 metres, was so badly damaged by falling rocks in 2010 that it had to be closed – just a few months after it was first opened. Following the closure of that bridge, hikers on the route were forced to go down around 800 metres into the valley, and climb back up again on the other side. This represented an enormous detour – but one which the new pedestrian suspension bridge means no longer has to be travelled. The bridge owes its name to its main sponsor, a businessman from Wallis.

The building of this highly advanced construction took around three months to complete. There are no bridge piers along the route. Instead, the foundations on both sides are anchored up to 11 metres deep into the stone. They bear the total weight of 58 tonnes. From peak to peak, two strong steel ropes stretch across the valley. Iron rods mounted on to these every three metres hold the narrow grid on which hikers walk. Special absorbers ensure that the bridge doesn't vibrate too strongly. Even so, most people probably go a bit weak in the knees when crossing – it's best not to look down, but simply enjoy the unique mountain panorama all around instead.

Address 3928 Randa, Switzerland | Getting there Train from Bern via Visp to Randa, then around a two-hour hike to the bridge | Hours May–Oct, dependent on weather conditions, closed in winter for safety reasons | Tip The whole of the Europaweg is almost 40 kilometres long. In two one-day stages, it leads from Grächen via Randa to Zermatt. There are good views of the Matterhorn on several occasions.

78__Álfaskólinn
The only elf school

Huldufólk – the hidden people – is what Icelanders call elves, trolls, gnomes and other creatures. They are said to live everywhere: in stones, by lakes or near hot springs. They are the patron saints of nature on the island. It is up to them whether or not they reveal themselves to people. Even though they remain invisible for most, according to surveys, more than half of the Icelandic population believe in their existence.

Perhaps it's Iceland's magical landscape, into which fantastical beings fit all too well. Bizarre fields of lava and active volcanoes, huge glaciers, spraying geysers and majestic waterfalls: the island seems like the perfect backdrop for a fantasy film.

In fact, elves, trolls and the like play a big role here. If a new road is being planned, for example, the Ministry of Construction contacts experts who check whether there might be an elf settlement along the proposed route. There have been such cases all too often in the past when bulldozers have suddenly stopped working, or excavator shovels mysteriously broke. Many Icelanders are convinced: the hidden people defend themselves when the humans advance too recklessly into nature. As a result, it is not unknown for building plans to be changed following such incidents.

If you want to find out more about the Huldufólk, then Magnús Skarphéðinsson is the right man for you. This historian has been fascinated by these invisible creatures for many years, and passes on his knowledge at the elf school. Here, it is possible to learn everything about the 13 different types of elf, the difference between dwarves and trolls, or the behaviour of fairies. Lessons also include trips to places where the creatures are said to live. A course at the elf school won't mean you'll suddenly be able to see fairies and trolls – that remains up to them – but you will have learnt a lot about their hidden world, and about respecting nature.

Address Síðumúli 31, 108 Reykjavík, Iceland | **Getting there** Bus to Fellsmúli (lines 4, 11) or Grensás (lines 2, 14, 15, 17, 102) | **Hours** Three- to four-hour courses every Fri from 3pm | **Tip** The tourist office in Reykjavík has maps on which elf settlements and gnome tunnels are marked, so you can walk on the trail of the invisible creatures yourself.

79__Rīgas Centrāltirgus
The largest food market

2014 was a special year for Riga. As the European Capital of Culture, the Latvian metropolis was in the international spotlight. The city celebrated itself and its cultural diversity with an extensive programme of concerts, exhibitions and other events. During the opening days a rather unusual place also took centre stage: Riga's central market. Suddenly a colourful culture programme was on offer between the cooling counters and sales stands.

This is an indication of the importance of the Rīgas Centrāltirgus to the city. When it was opened in 1930, the market, covering 72,000 square metres, was not only the largest in Europe, but also the most modern. The Latvian Hanseatic city was the most important trading centre in the region, and Riga was often referred to as the 'pearl of the Baltic'.

Today it is mainly locals that shop here. You can find everything for your daily needs in the five gigantic halls – from local specialities to products from all around the world. The selection is huge: in one of the halls, fish lovers can choose between fresh carp, Norwegian herring and vast amounts of smoked mackerel, while in the next hall huge varieties of cheese are on offer. Particularly popular is *Jāņu siers*, a caraway cheese typical of Latvia. You can also try other regional products at the market, such as healthy birch juice or sweet and savory *Pankuki* – Latvian pancakes.

The 'belly of the city' has much to offer. The architecture of the market halls is also worth seeing, as they were made from the hangars of a former Zeppelin factory. The factory was located around 200 kilometres outside Riga, and had been built by the Germans during the First World War. In 1919, the area fell to Latvia, and the airship halls were subsequently used for the construction of the central market. Rīgas Centrāltirgus is therefore not just a market – it is also a piece of Latvian history.

Address Nēģu iela 7, 1050 Riga, Latvia | Getting there Tram to Centrāltirgus (lines 2, 3, 5, 7, 9 and 10) | Hours Daily 7am – 6pm | Tip The former warehouse district of Spīķeri near the market halls is developing into an artist's quarter, with studios, galleries and cafés, and is certainly worth a detour.

80 Polar Night Light Festival

The most northerly light festival

It is the middle of the night, and winter has the small town of Ruka in Finnish Lapland in its cold, firm grip. Yet the ski lifts are as busy as they can be. During the Polar Night Light Festival, the pistes are flooded with colourful light, and the skiers – equipped with torches, headband lights and reflectors – become part of a brilliant work of art.

Ruka is one of the most important centres for winter sports in Finland. It is located near the Arctic Circle, almost 800 kilometres from the country's capital, Helsinki. The ski season begins in mid-October, and continues right through to May. 34 slopes, 22 lifts and around 200 days of guaranteed snow attract many winter holidaymakers every year, with major international competitions in ski jumping, cross-country skiing or Nordic combination also taking place here.

The long winter in Ruka is also a dark time, however, especially in December and January, when the sun in northern Lapland is visible for only a few hours each day. But since 2017 the Polar Night Light Festival has brought around two weeks of colourful light into this period of darkness. Dozens of installations by Nordic light artists ensure that the snow-covered landscape around the town is imaginatively illuminated. Visitors admire the works of art both on the pistes and in the village itself. There is great variety, from abstract projections to ultraviolet paintings in luminous neon shades. To enable the light art to be fully appreciated, neon signs on shops and restaurants are turned off for the duration of the festival.

With a winter landscape straight out of a fairytale storybook, the small Finnish town of Ruka is certainly worth a visit at any time of the year, but the light-art festival is a particular highlight – in the truest sense of the word.

Address Ruka, 93825 Kuusamo, Finland | Getting there Fly to Kuusamo, then it's around 40 minutes by bus to Ruka. | Hours Information on festival dates available from www.lightfestival.fi | Tip From September to February there's a good chance of seeing the Northern Lights in the region around Ruka.

81 Bolwoningen

The only settlement with spherical houses

At first you might think that UFOs have landed. And not only two or three, but a few dozen. But this is no alien invasion. The city of 's-Hertogenbosch, around 100 kilometres south of Amsterdam, is the location of one of the most unusual residential areas in Europe. 50 white, spherical houses stand in the middle of a typical Dutch suburb, surrounded by plain brown architecture from the 1980s. The globe-shaped buildings look like oversized mushrooms that have sprouted from the ground.

This eccentric housing project is called Bolwoningen – 'ball houses'. The quirky architecture was designed by Dutchman Dries Kreijkamp. He had the idea for the spherical constructions at the end of the 1970s, and a few years later they were realised within the framework of a programme for experimental living. For the artist, designer and architect, the round form was the most natural and organic shape possible. It is reported that he once said in an interview: 'We live on a sphere, we are born out of a sphere, so why shouldn't we live in a sphere?'

The occupants of the Bolwoningen have since been able to experience how it feels to live in a round house. With around 55 square metres of living space, these dwellings don't exactly offer spacious accommodation, but their inhabitants use it effectively nonetheless. The bedroom is in the ground floor of the buildings, directly above which is the bathroom, while the upper floor houses the living room and kitchen. Here, six circular windows ensure that space is flooded with light. Each of the spherical buildings stands on a concrete cylinder, which offers additional storage space. A sophisticated living concept in futuristic form.

Admittedly, finding the appropriate furnishings for a round house represents a bit of a challenge, but that's a price worth paying for the unique experience living in these residences.

Address Bollenveld, 5235 's-Hertogenbosch, The Netherlands | Getting there Around
one hour by train from Amsterdam to 's-Hertogenbosch, then bus line 9 to Bollenveld |
Tip Round forms seem to be omnipresent in 's-Hertogenbosch: you should definitely try
Bossche Bollen, a ball-shaped, cream-filled pastry!

82 ___ San Marino
The oldest republic

The fact that San Marino is a state in itself is often overlooked. That isn't particularly surprising considering that, with only 61 square kilometres of land, the country is one of the smallest in Europe. Yet it is also the oldest existing republic on the continent, as San Marino has always been independent.

Perhaps that has something to do with the country's location: completely surrounded by Italy, San Marino is hidden in the mountainous hinterland of Rimini. The Monte Titano, at roughly 740 metres, dominates the landscape. From its summit, it's possible to see the Adriatic Sea to the east, and the Apennines to the west. The fortifications on the rocks testify to the fact that the small republic has had to defend itself over the course of history.

The capital, San Marino Città, is also on the mountain. The only way up to the car-free old town, with its narrow alleyways and old ruins, is by cable car or on foot. The tomb of Saint Marinus, founder and namesake of the country, is located in the basilica. The stonemason is said to have fled from the persecution of Christians in Rimini up the Monte Titano. Here, the charismatic lay preacher laid the foundations for the republic that still exists to day. Even though few sources from this time have survived, the year 301 is considered the date of its foundation making the mini-state the oldest republic in the world.

There was never a king in San Marino. Nowadays, two 'Capitani Reggenti' elected by the parliament share power in the Palazzo Pubblico, for six months at a time. A re-election straight after is precluded, so that no one remains at the head of the state for too long.

'I leave you free from both men', the founder of the republic is believed to have said on his death bed, referring to the Roman Emperor and the Pope. It is this spirit of independence that has characterised San Marino for more than 1,700 years.

Address San Marino Città, 47890 San Marino | **Getting there** San Marino is around 30 kilometres from Rimini, with regular buses taking around 30 minutes. | **Tip** The border between Italy and San Marino is – as in many places in Europe – invisible, but if you want a special souvenir, you can get your passport stamped at the tourist office.

83 __ Chá Gorreana

The oldest tea plantation

They are not much further from the American continent as they are from the European mainland: the Azores – a lonely outpost of Portugal in the mid-Atlantic. But it is not only the location of the islands that is special. There is never a frost here, with the climate mild and humid all year round. Broad parts of the island group have thus developed into a lush, evergreen paradise. Colourful blossoming hydrangea bushes grow in the fertile volcanic soil, as well as sugar cane and tobacco – and also: tea!

There are various stories about how tea first got to the Azores. One tells of a Portuguese commander, who is said to have brought the plants with him from Brazil; another names two Chinese men who visited the Atlantic islands in 1878. Whatever the truth, the import was a blessing for the islanders, as tea growing became an important source of income on the Azores for many decades. In its heyday there were a total of 62 plantations.

The oldest still existing is Chá Gorreana, located in the north of São Miguel island. Tea has been grown here since 1883, and it is managed by the Mota family in the fifth generation. Many of the machines used for harvesting and processing the leaves are the same as those used in the early days, and many steps in the process are still performed by hand.

Tourists can find out how for themselves, with a visit to the plantation. April to September is harvest time. After picking, the tea leaves are taken to the factory, where they are sorted by hand, and go on to dry and ferment. Between 30 and 40 tonnes of black and green tea are produced here every year.

Tea from the Azores cannot keep up with the competition from India or Sri Lanka in terms of price, but the owners of Chá Gorreana don't let that discourage them. They plan to continue exporting tea from Europe's oldest plantation all around the world.

Address Plantações de Chá Gorreana, 9625-304 Maia, São Miguel, Azores, Portugal | **Getting there** Fly to Ponta Delgada on São Miguel, then it's around 30 minutes by rental car to the tea plantation in the north of the island. | **Hours** Mon–Fri 8am–6pm, Sat & Sun 9am–6pm | **Tip** On a guided tour you'll find out about the process of tea growing, and can try different varieties.

84 Schlangenfarm Schladen
The biggest snake farm

Jürgen Hergert has always had a passion for snakes. And without him and his love of these fascinating creatures, there certainly wouldn't be a snake farm in Schladen, in Lower Saxony. As a child, Hergert lived in Namibia for several years, and later his job as a mechanical engineer took him back to Africa again and again. There he learned how to handle the reptiles on a snake farm in Johannesburg, South Africa. In due course he studied zoology, and then decided to open his own snake farm in Germany. His love of snakes became a career – and a one-of-a-kind project in Europe.

The farm has been in existence for around 40 years, even though Jürgen Hergert no longer runs it himself. Having caught the first animals for himself in the wild, today the farm is home to around 60 species from various regions of the world, and houses a total of around 1,300 exotic animals, many of which are highly poisonous. As well as snakes, there are also scorpions, turtles, piranhas and monitor lizards in Schladen. Visitors can discover them all on a walk around the attraction, and learn a lot of interesting facts about the animal inhabitants at the daily presentations. It's also possible to tackle any fear of touching them you might have!

Visitors are only allowed to handle the harmless animals of course. Anything else would be too risky – Hergert knew that only too well, as his own life was once in danger after he was bitten by a black mamba. But that didn't stop him from continuing to dedicate himself to his pet project.

Incidentally, the snake farm also makes an important contribution to medical research: the snakes are regularly 'milked' with antiserums and medicines made from the poison they provide. These are used in the treatment of rheumatism, gout and high blood pressure all around the world – all thanks to Jürgen Hergert and his enduring fascination for snakes.

Address Im Gewerbegebiet 5, 38315 Schladen-Werla, Germany | Getting there Train from Hannover via Braunschweig to Schladen, then a walk of around 25 minutes to the snake farm on the edge of town | Hours Daily Nov–Feb 10am–5pm, Mar–Oct 10am–4pm | Tip From Schladen it is only about an hour by car to the famous mountain Brocken in the popular low mountain range Harz.

85 Schwyz-Stoos-Bahn
The steepest funicular

The small Swiss village of Stoos is a popular holiday destination. The 150-person community sits in an idyllic location on a plateau at around 1,300 metres above sea level, surrounded by the Alpine summits of Schwyz canton. It is not that easy to visit this car-free village, however: Stoos can only be reached by one of the local cable cars. The most spectacular approach, though, is via the Schwyz-Stoos-Bahn.

The funicular, with its four glass cabins that look like large barrels, has been conveying locals and tourists from the valley station of Schlattli to the mountain village of Stoos since the end of 2017. On the roughly 1.75-kilometre route, the train rises almost 750 metres. This was no easy task for the engineers, with planning and construction on the route taking many years. The maximum gradient in some sections is, believe it or not, 110 per cent. This means that for every 100 metres of horizontal movement, the wagons travel vertically for 110 metres. To ensure that the journey is as comfortable as possible, the cylindrical cabins continually turn and adapt to the respective incline, while the floor upon which the passengers stand remains level at all times. In this way it's possible to enjoy the view of the mountain landscape through the glass windows for the entire route.

The trip from the valley station up on to the mountain takes only a few minutes. During the journey the funicular passes through three tunnels as it climbs ever higher. In the upper tunnel, the illuminated statue of Saint Barbara, the patron saint of miners and tunnel workers, watches over events. Once you have passed through the last tunnel, the landscape levels out, and a little time later you arrive in Stoos – the mountain village that has obtained not only an important mode of transport with the new funicular, but also an extraordinary record.

Address Grundstrasse 230, 6430 Schwyz, Switzerland | Getting there Train from Lucerne to Schwyz, continue by bus (line 1) to the funicular valley station | Hours Timetable information is available at www.stoos-muotatal.ch | Tip Around Stoos there are many hiking and climbing tours in the summer months, while 35 kilometres of pistes attract skiers in winter.

86__Etna

The tallest active volcano

Etna is constantly grumbling within its rocky depths – and some-times this ancient volcano in north-east Sicily roars, glowing lava and masses of hot rock erupting from the earth in a spectacle of immense natural power. The fountains of lava can shoot up several hundred metres into the air, before falling to the ground in the surrounding landscape on the Italian island.

There's a fine line between fascination and danger with Etna. That has always been the case. The first eruptions occurred more than half a million years ago, since when the volcano has demonstrated its power on countless occasions, sometimes destroying whole villages and cities with its liquid rock in the process. The area surrounding Etna seems like the surface of the moon, strewn with huge craters and black boulders.

Yet this is not a static environment, as the picture changes signif-icantly with every eruption. The fire-breathing mountain grows or shrinks as rocks shift on the edge of the crater. The summit towers more than 3,300 metres above sea level, making Etna the tallest cur-rently active volcano in Europe.

Sicilians have got used to life under constant threat of eruption. After all, the volcano is also a blessing for the Mediterranean island and its residents. The volcanic rock stores water like a sponge, and the soils are mineralised and fertile. As a result, this part of Sic-ily transforms into a green oasis, especially in spring. Pistachio and almond trees alternate with lemon groves and blossoming meadows of flowers, and many vineyards have also located themselves around Etna, as the soil gives the grapes an intense, mineral taste. Without the volcano, those aromatic Sicilian wines that provide many people with both pleasure and an income would not exist. So while those who live in the shadow of Etna respect its irrepressible power, they also appreciate its gifts.

Address Etna, Sicily, Italy | **Getting there** Fly to Catania, then take a rental car or coach to one of the two mountain stations which are the starting points for tours. Depending on the volcano's acitity, parts may be closed off. | **Tip** Experience the volcano from a different perspective with the historic narrow gauge railway Ferrovia Circumetnea. The route leads from Catania to Riposto in almost a full circumnavigation of Etna.

87 __ High Tatras
The smallest high mountain region

The High Tatras are in many respects a special mountain range. They span two countries, with two-thirds of the area belonging to Slovakia, one-third to Poland. This small mountain range is a maximum of 50 kilometres long and 15 kilometres wide, but offers an impressive alpine landscape, with 25 of its peaks more than 2,500 metres tall. You'll also find the last Sherpas in Europe here.

In the Slovakian part of the High Tatras, load-carrying has tradition. The mountain cabins are not yet accessible by cable car or road, so on foot is the only option. Everything needed to care for guests has to be carried to the top – from food and drinks to building materials, to pots and gas cylinders for cooking. The Slovakian sherpas balance their loads on traditional wooden frames when walking up the narrow, stony paths, carrying up to 100 kilograms at once – a back-breaking job!

The fact that the summit is so difficult to reach is a stroke of luck for nature, however, as major parts of the High Tatras remain largely untouched. Alongside lynxes, martens and marmots, wolves and bears are also at home in the region. On both sides of the border the mountains are protected as national parks, and hikers can find peace and space to recuperate between clear lakes, roaring waterfalls and rustic huts – often far away from mass tourism.

More life returns to the small mountain range during the winter months, which see the High Tatras become a Mecca for winter sports. For Slovakia, it is the biggest skiing area in the country. On the Polish side most visitors are attracted to Zakopane at the foot of the national park. From there they take the cable car to the ski pistes at an altitude of almost 2,000 metres.

Whether winter or summer, those visiting the High Tatras for the first time will be absolutely amazed at everything the small area of high mountains has to offer.

Getting there On the Slovakian side the High Tatras are most easily accessed via Poprad (by plane or train), on the Polish side via Zakopane, by trains or car from Cracow. | Tip There is also plenty to discover on the 'inside' of the High Tatras, as the region possesses several stalactite caves. The largest, Belianska jaskyňa, is in Slovakia, around 30 kilometres from Poprad.

88__Longyearbyen
The northernmost settlement

Beware: polar bears! When you approach the edge of Longyearbyen, this stark warning leaps out from official signposts. And it is no joke: on the archipelago surrounding the Norwegian island of Spitsbergen there are many more polar bears than there are people. For safety reasons tourists are only allowed to leave the town accompanied by an armed guide. Longyearbyen itself is a small piece of civilisation in the middle of the Arctic Ocean. A visit to the northernmost permanently inhabited settlement in Europe is therefore a truly extreme experience.

Mountains, glaciers and barren landscape dominate the scenery for as far as the eye can see. There are no trees, and in fact hardly any green vegetation at all. Longyearbyen lies at a latitude of 78 degrees north, around half way between the Norwegian mainland and the North Pole, and belongs to the archipelago Svalbard. Between the end of October and the middle of February the sun no longer makes it over the horizon on this group of islands, which spend months deep in the polar night. Unsurprisingly, it's also cold: even in midsummer the temperatures here rarely climb above 5 °C.

But none of this daunts the roughly 2,100 inhabitants of the former mining town – nor those tourists who find their way here. You feel nature more closely, more directly and more pristinely here than in any other place in Europe. The region around Longyearbyen offers an abundance of unique experiences. In winter you can go on an expedition by snowmobile or dogsled, while in summer its possible to take several-day hikes on the glaciers. Or you can travel by boat to the impressive icebergs in the nearby fjords, where whales can often be observed. Sometimes you can even see the dance of the Northern Lights in the night sky. And if you are even luckier, you might get to see the king of the Arctic on one of your trips near Longyearbyen: the polar bear. But please: always keep your distance!

Address Longyearbyen, Spitsbergen, Norway | **Getting there** Travel to Longyearbyen by air or boat from Oslo or Tromsø | **Tip** At Gruvelageret restaurant in a former warehouse you can trace the tracks of Longyearbyen's mining past. The Norwegian royal family has also dined here.

89 Olympia Bob Run

The only naturally refrigerated bob run

The cold flow of air in your face, the world roaring past in a speeding blur. Your heart races, your knees turn to jelly. Four times your normal body weight keeps you pinned in your seat, and you are hurled from left to right and back again in the tight corners as you descend the channel of ice at speeds of more than 130 kilometres an hour. A guest ride on the Olympia Bob Run St. Moritz-Celerina is 75 seconds of pure adrenalin, and an experience that you won't forget in a hurry.

And what an extraordinary location for it, here in the Swiss Alps, where the bobsleigh was invented. In order to entertain a couple of bored Englishmen on their winter holiday, at the end of the 19th century a resourceful hotelier had two sledges welded together. The first ice run was built between St Moritz and the nearby town of Celerina in 1904, so that the crazy tourists didn't have to toboggan on the streets. And so the tradition began. To this day the course is remade in the same place every year. The run builders begin their work after the first snowfall, then build the new bob run over a period of three weeks using diggers and spades. This makes it not only the oldest run in the world, but also the only one that is made solely of ice and snow – without concrete foundation. The 1,700-metre-long track is built out of around 15,000 cubic metres of snow and 10 million litres of water.

Plenty of world cup champions and Olympians have whooshed down the famous ice run over the decades. But hobby bobsleighers are not left to their own fate on a guest ride. That would just be too risky given the high speeds. The rapid adventure is embarked upon in the four-man bob, passengers protected between pilot and brakeman, to ensure that every tourist reaches the bottom in one piece. You don't need to have any prior experience – but you will need a decent portion of derring-do!

Address Via Maistra 54, 7500 St Moritz, Switzerland | **Getting there** From St Moritz station bus 3 to St Moritz village, then bus 2 or 6 to St Moritz Bären | **Hours** Daily 7am–5pm, mid-Dec to early Mar | **Tip** In the nearby bob museum you can find out about the history of the sport and the bob run (Giassa da Scoula 6, 7505 Celerina).

90 — Royal National City Park

The first national park in a metropolis

Nature is never very far away in Stockholm. The Swedish capital is spread across 14 islands, and as a result there is water nearby wherever you might be. In addition to this, there is an abundance of green spaces throughout the city. Since 1995 it has also had the first national park in the heart of a metropolis in the world.

Almost 30 square kilometres of protected natural and cultural landscape are spread over parts of the city, all the way to the municipality of Solna in the north of Stockholm. The area is as diverse as it is large. The Baroque Ulriksdal park makes up the northern spur, while a little closer to the city centre is the English landscaped park of Haga, with its famous palace, the residence of Crown Princess Victoria. The Fjäderholmarna islands, south of the city at the start of the Stockholm archipelago, also belong to the national park.

But the heart of the national park area is Djurgården, the 'animal garden'. This area was once the exclusive hunting grounds of the Swedish royal family, but today it is open to the general public. Although the vast recreation area on the island of the same name is only a stone's throw from the city centre, it's possible to encounter foxes, herons and even elks here.

It's not only nature that makes the Djurgården so popular, however: some of the most-visited museums in the city are also located here. You might take a journey in time through the history of Sweden at the popular Skansen open-air museum. Not far away you could also explore the famous warship *Vasa* from the 17th century. And ABBA fans can also get their fill at Djurgården – along with guaranteed earworm – at the museum dedicated to Sweden's most famous and successful pop group.

Stockholm's Royal National City Park brings together nature and culture, right in the middle of the Swedish capital, and offers a refuge for locals and tourists alike.

Address 11521 Stockholm, Sweden | **Getting there** The park is easy to reach by public transport (bus, metro, boat). In summer, exploring the park by bike is recommended. | **Tip** You can also discover the Royal National City Park as part of a hop-on-hop-off boat tour. Large parts of the park are on the water. You can access most of them from the boat stops.

91 Tunnelbana
The longest underground art gallery

If you miss the metro in Stockholm, the irritation quickly fades, as in the stations of the Tunnelbana, deep beneath the Swedish capital, there is a lot to discover. The large majority of Stockholm's underground stations were designed by artists. Sculptures, mosaics, installations and murals make each of them a work of art, and the metro journey becomes a visit to a huge, subterranean art gallery.

The green light was given for the unusual project back at the end of the 1950s. The creative classes in Stockholm demanded more art in public locations, and the metro seemed to be the perfect place: easily accessible, open to everyone, and yet very well protected from wind and weather.

The T-Centralen station was the first to be transformed into a work of art. Large parts of the station are now dark blue, as the colour is claimed to radiate calm. Because the stop is the hub of the Stockholm metro system, and therefore especially busy, it seemed the perfect place for this calming shade. Floral patterns and rural motifs, also in soft blue, complement the image. Like many of Stockholm's underground stations, T-Centralen is hewn into the rock like a cave, which means visitors are enclosed by art.

Today, 94 of the 100 Tunnelbana stations are walk-in works of art. An underground garden seems to have spread through the Kungsträdgården station, while a green coniferous forest decorates the walls of the Solna Centrum station, over which the cave ceiling hovers like a luminous red sky. The entrance to the platform of the Stadion station is spanned by a huge rainbow. And the Thorildsplan stop is reminiscent of the 1980s world of computer games, with pixelated motifs from *Super Mario* and *Pac-Man*.

A trip on the metro in Stockholm is like a journey through the art styles of past decades – offering an interesting and attractive environment for anyone travelling through the city.

Address Stockholm, Sweden | Hours Mon–Thu 5am–1am, Fri & Sat 24 hours, Sun 6am–1am | Tip To find out more about the individual stations and works of art, take part in one of the regular guided tours, or download the SL ArtGuide smartphone app. The audio guide offers information on 21 stations in English and Swedish.

92 Hermitage

The museum with the largest art collection

Long queues form on Palace Square in front of the entrance to the Hermitage's main complex from early in the morning. The museum is one of St Petersburg's most important sights. More than four million tourists from all around the world visit the Russian city on the Neva every year in order to see the famous art treasures. They wait patiently to be admitted in front of the distinctive green and white facade of the Winter Palace. Once inside, a real art marathon begins.

Around 60,000 exhibits are displayed in the rooms of the Hermitage. Some three million more objects are stored in the archives. It is an enormous collection, the roots of which stretch back to Empress Catherine II. The German on the Russian tsar throne bought many important paintings, sculptures and drawings in the 18th century. In order to present them, several buildings around the Tsar's Palace were created over the course of time. Today, the Old, New and Small Hermitages as well as the Hermitage Theatre and the Winter Palace form a connected complex.

In many rooms, top-class works are lined up side by side. There are more than 350 halls full of art for visitors to discover. This includes paintings by famous masters such as Leonardo da Vinci, Picasso, Rembrandt and van Gogh. But the Hermitage also houses archaeological treasures, Roman statues, and lots of ornamentation and splendour from the tsar era. You will only manage to see a fraction of the content in a single visit. And even the magnificent halls and corridors of the museum are worth a second look. If you were to dedicate only 30 seconds to each of the works of art, you would have to spend almost three weeks in the Hermitage – twenty-four hours a day. That means there's only one thing for it: you'll have to return, and again join the queue in front of the bright green and white of the Winter Palace.

Address Palace Square 2, St Petersburg, 190000 Russia | Getting there Metro line 5 to Admiralteyskaya, from there just a few minutes' walk | Hours Tue, Thu, Sat & Sun 10.30am–6pm, Wed & Fri 10.30am–9pm | Tip The standard ticket gives access to most parts of the Hermitage, but you need to be part of a guided tour to visit the Treasure Gallery, with its many precious objects of gold and diamonds.

93 __ Pomnik Chrystusa Króla
The largest statue of Christ

Apparently it all began with an epiphany. Sylwester Zawadzki, the priest of the small Polish city of Świebodzin at the time, heard the Lord's call to build a memorial to him. So Zawadzki did everything he could to make this wish a reality. He secured a piece of land from the commune, had drawings and blueprints designed, and collected the necessary finances. The result can already be seen from the nearby motorway: the largest statue of Christ, not only in Europe, but in the entire world.

A 400-tonne colossus of concrete, wire, foam and plastic, the figure is 36 metres tall, with its arms spread benevolently over the Polish congregation. This means it even tops the famous sculpture in Rio de Janeiro by six metres. On the head of the saviour stands a massive golden crown. The measurements of the figure have a symbolic character. The size of the body – 33 metres – represents the 33 years that Christ is thought to have lived, the height of the crown – three metres – symbolises the three years of his public work, while at the feet of the statue are five stone circles, each representing one of the five continents.

That the huge figure was created in Poland of all places is also due to the fact that the Catholic Church is stronger in this country than in most other European states. Faith is an intrinsic part of Poles' everyday life, especially in small cities and towns. Although the project was not without controversy due to the huge costs, the vision of Zawadzki, who has since died, landed on fertile ground.

The monumental statue of Christ was inaugurated in 2010. It is intended to protect the citizens of Świebodzin, and secure them the favour of God. But many in the city – beyond all sacred thoughts – also link the monument with very secular hopes: the statue is likely to attract tourists and pilgrims, who will bring their money, and thus increase the city's wealth.

Address Sulechowska, 66–200 Świebodzin, Poland | **Getting there** By car, Świebodzin is on the A 2 motorway connecting Berlin and Warsaw, around 70 kilometres from the German border; by train it is over four hours from Warsaw, and two hours from Berlin. | **Tip** Not far from the statue is the Sanktuarium Miłosierdzia Bożego, an imposing church that was also built on the initiative of priest Zawadzki.

94__Tabernas Desert
The driest region

The sun burns mercilessly down from the sky, even in the morning, and the sandy ground is as hot as glowing coals. A horse and cart clatter by, a cowboy approaches from the distance on horseback, and the saloon doors creak in the dry desert wind. No, this is not the Wild West. This is not even the USA. We are in fact in the south of Spain, more precisely, in Andalusia.

The Tabernas Desert begins around 30 kilometres north of Almería. The area, which is strictly speaking only a semi-desert, covers an area of around 280 square kilometres. The sun shines here for more than 3,000 hours a year. In the summer, temperatures easily climb to 35 – 40 °C, and it is rare for more than 250 millimetres of rain to fall – in an entire year! As a result there are not many animals or plants. But that is precisely the potential of the region. With its barren landscape it has already served many directors as a backdrop for various adventure films. Around 500 movies have been made in Tabernas. Arnold Schwarzenegger transformed into Conan the Barbarian here, while Harrison Ford became Indiana Jones. Even part of the classic desert epic *Lawrence of Arabia* was filmed in the Spanish province.

But Tabernas Desert most often transforms into the Wild West. Charles Bronson and Henry Fonda fought out a duel here for Sergio Leone's cult Western *Once Upon a Time in the West*, Clint Eastwood got into several shoot-outs with bad guys for *A Fistful of Dollars*, and Pierre Brice stood in front of the camera in Tabernas Desert for the German TV production *Winnetous Rückkehr*. Elaborate sets were built for many of the productions, and at one point there were 14 such Western cities. Three of these are still standing today, and if there is no filming taking place, they are open to visitors. They then get the chance to feel like they're in the Wild West too – albeit in the middle of Europe.

Address Tabernas Desert, Almería Province, 04200 Spain | Getting there From Almería you can reach Tabernas by car in half an hour. | Tip Visit the backdrop town Fort Bravo (daily 9am–7.30pm), which still serves as a film location today. Visitors can experience stuntmen performing daily Western shows.

95__Silfra fissure

The only diving spot between two continents

There's a crack running through the world of the Icelanders. It crosses the whole island – and has left clear marks behind it in many places. This is because Iceland sits on the seam between the Eurasian and North American continental plates. Every year the two plates drift a little further apart, and this movement has created a trench that shapes the Icelandic landscape to some extent.

In Thingvellir National Park in the south-west region of the island, an internationally unique spot for divers and snorkellers has been formed by this rift: the Silfra fissure. Filled with the ice-cold melt water of the Langjökull glacier, it runs like a narrow stream through the flat landscape. Those who want to enter the water here need some courage – and good equipment. Even in summer the water temperature is only a few degrees, and can be endured for more than a couple of minutes only if wearing a special dry suit. And even then divers' fingers quickly become numb, and the cold results in an unpleasant stinging of the face.

But despite the discomfort, diving into this unique underwater world is certainly a worthwhile endeavour. The icy glacier water flows through filtering lava rock for years before it reaches Silfra. The water is crystal clear, cleaner than anywhere else. It's so clear you could easily forget that you are under water. From the surface it's even possible to make out the floor, which is more than 60 metres away at the deepest point. You can therefore see the angular rock faces that fall away razor sharp on both sides. The world in the deep glimmers, sometimes bright blue, sometimes emerald green, but always mysterious.

There are no fish, plants or even corals to discover in the fissure. Instead, you can spread out your arms when diving in one of the narrower parts, and touch a different continent on each side – an absolutely unique experience.

Address Thingvellir National Park, 801 Selfoss, Iceland | Getting there The national park is around 50 kilometres from Reykjavík. | Tip Even in summer you can only dive or snorkel the Silfra fissure with a dry suit, but you need the respective certificate for dives. Snorkel and diving trips often start from the car park near Silfra.

96__Guédelon
The largest medieval castle building project

The Guédelon building site is always very busy. There's hammering, sawing and work going on all around. After all, a whole castle is to be built here – a castle as it would have looked in the Middle Ages, surrounded by a fortification wall, with guard towers and a moat. When you look a little closer, however, you realise that not only should the building appear as if it were made in the Middle Ages, the handicraft technologies being used are also anything but modern.

It is surely one of the most unusual building projects in the whole of Europe. Guédelon castle near the French village of Treigny is being made exclusively using methods and materials that date back to the early 13th century. As a result, every stone for the building is hewn from the nearby quarry, and then formed into the right shape by hand by stonemasons. Every single nail and every tool is forged on site using traditional means. Even the pigments in the paint workshop for decorating the walls are extracted directly from earth and ground stone. It is an often exhausting and especially time-consuming job for the roughly 40 craftsmen working here. They have been building since 1997, and there is no end in sight.

Despite this, it is worth the effort. The project also pursues a scientific approach. Historians and archaeologists were as involved from the beginning as the architects who designed the structure. Through the construction, many long-forgotten techniques have been rediscovered.

The numerous tourists who visit the building site can literally immerse themselves in the world of the Middle Ages here. The admission fees they pay chiefly finance the ambitious plans of the initiators. And if you want to make a physical contribution, you can sign on at Guédelon as a voluntary helper for a couple of days – and thus play your own small part in the largest medieval castle building project in Europe.

Address 89520 Treigny, France | Getting there Guédelon is around 10 kilometres from the town of Treigny on the D955. The nearest railway station is Cosne-sur-Loire, from which it is a half-hour drive to the building site. | Hours Mid-Mar – early Nov; more information available at www.guedelon.fr | Tip If you want to volunteer on the building site, you must apply in advance, and should be able to speak French.

97__Eble Clock Park
The biggest cuckoo clock

Why, of all things, a cuckoo, with its typical call, should be used to announce the time remains an enigma to this day. Apparently a clockmaker in the 18th century was working on an alarm clock with the crow of a cock, but struggled to replicate the 'cock-a-doodle-doo' with its five tones. Thus he exchanged the cock for a cuckoo. Whether this is true is unclear – as is the answer to the question of where the cuckoo clock was actually invented. Today, in any case, it belongs quite firmly to the Black Forest region – just like cherry cake and the traditional hats called Bollenhut. The ornate wooden box with clockwork, pendulum, weights and cuckoo stands as a symbol for tradition and German craftsmanship around the world.

Watchmaker Ewald Eble, from the small town of Triberg, is also a master of this craft. His family has been producing clocks since 1880. Together with his son Ralf he has designed a very special model: the biggest cuckoo clock in the world. It is 60 times bigger than the traditional version, as tall as a real house. The clockwork alone measures 4.50 by 4.50 metres. Meanwhile, the massive wooden cuckoo, that appears at the window on the first floor every half an hour, weighs a stately 150 kilograms. It took the two masters five years to complete. Everything was made by hand using traditional methods, as the clock was to work mechanically, just like the classic small version.

The huge clock in Triberg is now a magnet for visitors. While for a long time cuckoo clocks were considered the epitome of parochialism and kitsch, in the meantime something of a cult has grown around them. Whether with carved wooden figures, plain and linear or colourful and trendy, they are now more widely sought after than any other souvenir, especially among foreign tourists. With every Black Forest cuckoo clock, a piece of Germany travels out into the wide world too.

Address Schonachbach 27, 78098 Triberg, Germany | Getting there By car, around 1.5 hours from Stuttgart, or by train, Triberg can be reached from Offenburg in 45 minutes, or Konstanz in 1.5 hours | Hours Mon–Sat 9am–6pm, Sun 10am–6pm (Easter–Oct), Mon–Sat 9am–5.30pm, Sun 11am–5pm (Nov–Easter) | Tip As well as the biggest, Triberg also has the smallest cuckoo clock in the world: the 13.5-centimetre version was built in Hubert Herr's factory (Hauptstraße 8).

98__Salina Turda

The lowest amusement park

You can't see particularly far, even when the gondola is at the highest point on the Ferris wheel. Nonetheless, it's a unique view, as this big wheel turns deep beneath the ground in the gallery of an abandoned salt mine. Salt hasn't been extracted from the Salina Turda mine in north-west Romania for around 90 years now, and where miners once toiled away in their labours, tourists now enjoy themselves in a subterranean amusement park.

The way down to the park, located up to 120 metres into the depths, is by lift or stairs. Several gallery tunnels and mines are open to visitors, and spectacular views that make the extent of the former mine clear are revealed time and again. The layers of salt in the stone can still be discerned on the illuminated walls, and occasionally impressive stalactites of salt extend downwards from the vaulted ceiling.

While the Romans had already mined salt in this region, the construction of a dedicated salt mine in Turda began in 1690. The mine was in operation up until the 1930s, after which it served as an air-raid shelter, and later as a cheese warehouse for some time, before being retired as a museum.

New life finally returned with the amusement park in 2010. Since then, visitors have been able to ride the Ferris wheel in the impressive Rudolf Mine or, a little deeper still in the Terezia Mine, paddle across a subterranean lake in a boat. In the middle of the lake an island has formed from salt residue, on which it's possible to spend time bowling or playing minigolf. There are also table tennis and pool tables at visitors' disposal. And if the park's attractions aren't of interest, you can at least console yourself in the knowledge that time spent in the mine is healthy, as the humid, saline air is good for the circulation and the airways. Fun times and healthy treatments come together naturally in Salina Turda.

Address Aleea Durgăului 7, 401106 Turda, Romania | **Getting there** The nearest airport is Cluj-Napoca, from which it is around 45 minutes to Turda by car or bus. | **Hours** Daily 9am–5pm | **Tip** You should dress up warm for a visit to the salt mine, even in summer, as it is only around 10–12 °C inside the mine all year round.

99__Ulm Minster
The highest steeple

You can see it from far off – the steeple of Ulm Minster is outstanding in the fullest sense of the word. It rises to just over 161 metres into the sky – higher than any other church tower in the world. It is the uncontested symbol of the city on the Danube.

The Gothic architecture, the 15-metre-tall church windows, the elaborate altars, the gigantic organ: almost everything about Ulm Minster is impressive. Just like the construction period. It took more than 500 years from the laying of the foundation stone in 1377 to its completion in 1890. The fact that the monumental evangelical house of God was built in the 130,000-person city in Baden-Württemberg, is thanks to the citizens of Ulm. The minster is a people's church – the building was financed completely by the residents of the city. The Ulm locals are thus suitably proud of their record-breaker to this day.

Incidentally, according to the legend there was animal help in the building of the church. The craftsmen were struggling to transport an especially large wooden beam for the minster transversely through the city gate. They were about to tear down the gate when a sparrow, which was carrying a twig lengthwise in its beak, is said to have flown through it. The solution dawned on them, and so the church could be built after all. In thanks, they created a monument to the little bird on the roof of the minster. The Ulm Sparrow is ubiquitous in the city to this day – whether in the form of a pastry or as a souvenir.

Most visitors come, of course, to experience the sublime feeling of climbing the highest steeple in the world. You can't go all the way to the top, but you can at least stand on the viewing platform at a height of 143 metres. Exactly 768 steps lead up the tower, but the view more than compensates for the strenuous ascent. It is – just like the minster itself – simply outstanding.

Address Münsterplatz 1, 89073 Ulm, Germany | **Getting there** Around 10 minutes' walk from Ulm main station | **Tip** In the 3D-flight simulator Birdly (Ulm Stories, Münsterplatz 25) you can experience Ulm Minster from a bird's-eye perspective with VR goggles. The simulator translates your arm movements into flaps, and you fly like a bird through the virtual streets around the minster.

100__ Valletta

The smallest capital

You're unlikely to get blisters walking the streets of Valletta. There aren't many capitals in Europe you can discover so comfortably on foot: the Maltese city is only around one kilometre long and a maximum of 600 metres wide. Yet it offers lots of sights and fascinating history for visitors.

Valletta juts from the blue of the Mediterranean like a fortress of yellow sandstone. Surrounded by thick ramparts, the city in the southeast of Malta is located on a peninsula. Locals often simply refer to Valletta as 'Il Belt' – 'the city'. It was knights of the Order of Saint John who built Valletta as a stronghold in the mid-16th century, in order to better protect the island against hostile attacks. The city got its name from the Grandmaster of the order, Jean Parisot de la Valette.

Inside the city walls the knights had sumptuous palaces and churches built, which still dominate the city's landscape to this day. Strolling through the narrow, chessboard alleys, you'll be astonished by the Baroque facades. You can also explore some of the grand buildings, such as the Grandmaster's Palace, once the stately residence of the city's founder.

Valletta's most important place of interest is also a relic of the Order of Saint John: St John's Co-Cathedral in the heart of the city. The church may seem plain from the outside, but appearances can be deceptive. Inside there are elaborate ceiling frescoes, framed by golden ornamentation, while the floor is embellished with ornate tomb slabs of the knights of the order. A real art treasure is hidden away in the oratorio: Caravaggio's masterpiece *The Beheading of John the Baptist*, dating from 1608.

The cathedral could be an allegory for the whole of Valletta. The Maltese capital is often underestimated due to its size. But if you look behind the plain sandstone walls, you'll be surprised at all the things the smallest capital in Europe has to offer.

Address Valletta, Malta | **Getting there** The island's airport is around 8 kilometres from Valletta, and bus X4 connects it to the capital. | **Tip** Valletta is small, but the paths are very steep in parts. If you're coming from the harbour and want to get to the cathedral, make life easier by using the Barrakka Lift, which will take you 58 metres up to the Upper Barrakka Gardens.

101__Pench's Bar

The bar with the biggest cocktail menu

We knew that the art of mixing a good cocktail is all about the details long before James Bond came to our attention, with his preference for a Martini shaken, not stirred. However, every good barkeeper would advise you against this: shaking a cocktail makes the drink cloudy and waters it down slightly. Nothing against James Bond, but real connoisseurs drink their Martini stirred and not shaken.

It's the small differences that account for a good cocktail. The bartenders in Pench's know that all too well, because here they specialise in mixed drinks. In the middle of the Bulgarian Black Sea metropolis of Varna, less than two kilometres from the popular beach, this bar offers an unrivalled selection of cocktails. With 2,014 alcoholic creations on its menu, founder Pencho Penchev currently holds the world record. He has worked constantly to develop new variations since the opening of the bar in 1995. Such is the passion here that the barkeepers from Pench's regularly outperform all others at international cocktail competitions.

The selection of drinks on offer ranges from classics such as the Margarita, Moscow Mule or Cosmopolitan, to more exotic alternatives such as the fruity 'Tiki Cocktails'. But you can also choose one of Pencho Penchev's own creations, most of which are aimed at the more adventurous tippler.

For example, Bartender's Blood is a mixture of gin, litchi liqueur, crème de cassis, cassis syrup and dry red wine. Or there's the Lifeguard cocktail, in which rum, lime juice and orange bitters are mixed with a little egg white. Also rather unusual are cocktails that mature in oak barrels, with six of these highly unconventional drinks on the menu at Pench's.

The fantasy of the Bulgarian barkeepers seems to know no limits. But you're welcome even if you aren't a cocktail fan: if you really must, you can always order a boring old beer.

Address Bulevard 8–mi Primorski Polk 119, 9002 Varna, Bulgaria | **Getting there** Varna has its own airport, from which bus 409 will take you into the city centre, where Pench's is located. | **Hours** Daily 7pm–2am | **Tip** Due to the limited capacity, Bulgarians who wish to visit Pench's must become members. Foreign guests have free access.

102__Vatican
The smallest country

The best views over the roofs of the Vatican are from the dome of the famous St Peter's Basilica. From here it is easily possible to look over the entire territory. With just around 44 hectares of land, the mini-state is only slightly larger than the Munich Oktoberfest site, and it's possible to walk around it in less than an hour. Built on the Monte Vaticano hill in the middle of the Italian capital, Rome, the Vatican, which is the seat of the Pope, has been an independent, sovereign state since 1929.

But it is not only the size of the Vatican that is unusual – this miniature country surprises visitors with numerous curiosities. For example, Latin, rather than Italian, is really the official language. The tiny state also has its own newspaper, a fire brigade, three post offices, and even its own football league. There is also a separate railway station, although this has only been used a couple of times by various Popes over the past decades.

The Vatican is protected by the Swiss Guard. Anyone wishing to be admitted into the small army, with its striking red, blue and yellow uniforms, has to meet certain criteria: they must be a Swiss citizen, of Catholic faith, fit, and at least 1.74 metres tall. Despite the omnipresent guards, the Vatican has one of the highest crime rates in the world. This is due to the countless pickpockets in relation to the low number of residents.

Thousands of tourists visit every day in order to view the famous St Peter's Basilica, the Sistine Chapel and the Vatican museums, or to participate in one of the Pope's weekly general audiences. He is not only the head of the Catholic Church, but also the secular leader in the Vatican. Although the area of his state is small, his power is great. All three powers are unified in his hand, and he can rule, once he is elected, for as long as he wishes. This also makes the mini-state of the Vatican Europe's last absolute monarchy.

Getting there The Vatican is in the centre of Rome on the west bank of the Tiber, and can be reached via numerous buses, on foot, or via the metro; the nearest station is Ottaviano (line A). | Tip If you'd like to visit St Peter's Basilica, check beforehand whether services or other events are planned on that day, in which case it will be closed.

103__ Vatnajökull
The biggest glacier

Warm jackets, gloves and walking boots with ice cleats are all part of the basic equipment required for a hike on the Vatnajökull. And don't forget the camera! A spectacular motif offers itself up every few metres when you're out and about on the eternal ice of Iceland. From gigantic glacier tongues and lagoons full of swimming icebergs, to waterfalls fed by meltwater, the dramatic landscape, which glows in shades from radiant white to azure blue, seems almost magical.

The Vatnajökull, located in the south-east region of Iceland, is made up of more than 3,000 cubic kilometres of ice. This makes it the glacier with the largest volume in Europe. If it were to melt, it would make the sea level around the entire world rise by about one centimetre. When Vatnajökull formed around 2,500 years ago, Iceland was almost completely covered in masses of ice. Glaciers have shaped the island, but today they are threatened by climate change. The first glacier on Iceland was declared dead in 2019.

In order to best preserve the Vatnajökull, it has been a protected site since 2008 as part of a national park. Visitors can explore it with the help of guides: on hikes, ice-climbing adventures, or tours through the ice caves. These cavities in glaciers are formed by meltwater. The layer of ice that encloses visitors is up to several hundred metres thick, and you can often hear crunching from the inside of the glacier, which is constantly moving. The walls of the caves shimmer in various shades – from bright blue to violet and black – a beautiful spectacle that makes the camera particularly important to remember!

A tour through the ice caves of Vatnajökull is a truly unique experience. In spring, when the temperatures rise, the caves often collapse and disappear – but they reform anew the next winter, so there are always new and beautiful images to capture.

Address Vatnajökull National Park, Iceland | **Getting there** The national park is around 330 kilometres from Reykjavík in south-east Iceland. Guided tours to Vatnajökull are possible from Reykjavík or Skaftafell on the edge of the national park. | **Hours** The ice caves are only accessible without danger to life between November and March. All other activities on Vatnajökull are possible all year round. | **Tip** A special attraction is the so-called crystal ice cave. Here the ice ceiling is so thin that the sunlight shines through it as if it were crystal.

104_Koncertzāle Latvija

The concert hall with the largest piano

A pianist having to climb a ladder to reach their instrument is a quite unusual proposition. In Koncertzāle Latvija, however, this is unavoidable. This is where the largest piano in the world is located: the M470i, a 4.7-metre-tall piano created by the German-Latvian piano builder David Klavins. In contrast to standard grand pianos, the instrument's body is not oriented horizontally, but vertically – almost as if the piano were standing on its head. The stairs are part of the instrument, and the pianist is positioned above the audience on a kind of balcony.

With its striking blue steel frame, the piano is permanently integrated into the new concert hall in the Latvian city of Ventspils. Having opened only in 2019, it is part of a modern music campus, with which the Baltic city hopes to become a port of call for those interested in music from all around the world. The proclaimed goal is to offer visitors new listening experiences.

Part of this concept is this unique piano. Klavins wanted to use longer strings, and the piano thus had to be correspondingly large. The strings are custom built, with the longest measuring 3.9 metres. This means the bass notes in particular sound more powerful, but nevertheless clear. The spruce soundboard is around two and a half times larger than in a normal concert piano, as a result of which it creates an especially full, sustained sound. The vertical design also has a purpose: the audience sits pretty much opposite the instrument, and is therefore directly in line with the sound waves it creates.

This is not the first piano of this kind that Klavins has built, and he continues to work on developing his instruments. Who knows what he will come up with next? In the meantime, everyone has the chance to experience the unusual sound of his giant piano – in the Latvija concert hall in Ventspils.

Address Koncertzāle Latvija, Lielais prospekts 1, 3601 Ventspils, Latvia | **Getting there**
The 200-kilometre bus journey from Riga to Ventspils takes around three hours, then it's
a 15-minute walk to the concert hall from the bus station. | **Hours** Information on concerts
at www.koncertzalelatvija.lv | **Tip** The predecessor model of the largest piano, the M450
by David Klavins, stands in the studio of the musician Nils Frahm in Berlin.

105__ Teatro Olimpico
The oldest theatre

You might believe you've accidentally stumbled on to the set of a period film when you enter Teatro Olimpico. Although it's not an open-air structure, the building is conceived like a Roman amphitheatre. It opened in 1585, as the first theatre of the modern era in Vicenza in northeastern Italy.

The building was designed by the Italian star architect of the Renaissance, Andrea Palladio, a son of the city. Classic Antiquity served him as a role model. And that is all too easy to recognise to this day. The tiered rows of seats lead steeply down to the stage in a semi-circle, and a colonnade lines the auditorium. But it is the stage design in particular that catches the visitor's eye. In the front section there is a monumental wall, evocative of the facades of Roman palaces. Through three portals it is possible to see the background constructions behind it: the illusion of an antique city, which, thanks to the clever play of perspective and light, achieves enormous apparent depth. It is the stylised city of Theben, setting of the drama *Oedipus Rex*, the first play ever to be staged here. The scenery – and this is the truly unbelievable part – has been preserved since the opening of the theatre almost 450 years ago.

Sophocles' drama about the prince of Theben, who kills his own father and takes his mother as his wife, is considered a masterpiece of antiquity. More than 2,000 years after its premiere, it offered the perfect material for the opening of Teatro Olimpico. Since then, the stage set has served as the backdrop for every performance and concert that has taken place here.

In order to protect the invaluable ancient constructions of wood and plaster, there are, however, only very few productions each year. In this way, the hope in Vicenza is that the oldest theatre of the modern era will be able to survive in all of its historical glory for many more years to come.

Address Piazza Matteotti 11, 36100 Vicenza, Italy | Getting there One-hour train journey from Venice to Vicenza, then a 15-minute walk to Teatro Olimpico | Hours Guided tours Tue–Sun 9am–5pm (Sept–June), 10am–6pm (July/Aug). Concerts and performances Apr–Oct only. More information at www.teatrolimpicovicenza.it | Tip In and around Vicenza you can view numerous other architectural masterpieces by Andrea Palladio – Villa Rotonda on the south-east edge of the city is especially impressive.

106__Red Force
The fastest roller coaster

Zero to 180 kilometres an hour in only five seconds – normally only Formula 1 racing drivers can achieve such acceleration. The Spanish amusement park PortAventura joined forces with the Italian sports car manufacturer Ferrari in order to make it possible for ordinary folk to experience this tremendous speed-up on a roller coaster. Red Force was the result of this collaboration, creating the fastest catapult roller coaster in Europe.

The wagons accelerate along a horizontal ramp in record time immediately after the start. A force of 4 g presses the occupants of Red Force back into their seats; this means that passengers' bodies feel four times their normal weight! Then you suddenly start to climb steeply, and the track turns upwards almost at right angles, the bright red roller coaster cars shooting vertically towards the sky. They climb 112 metres to the apex, before plummeting vertically back towards the earth. Although the rush of speed lasts only 30 seconds, in this time you've covered the 880-metre-long route. It's a short but intense kick.

Red Force is part of an entire Ferrari theme park. 16 attractions are collected on an area of around 70,000 square metres. Attractions range from Formula 1 simulators and a real racing track, to two drop towers that look like over-sized engine pistons. Meanwhile, for the children there is Junior Red Force – a miniature version of the record-breaking roller coaster.

The latter opened in 2017, and immediately stood out from the rest through its sheer size. More than 160 pillars support the colossus of steel and concrete. Its appearance alone is sufficient to cause most people's adrenalin levels to surge. This is the place to get the unique feeling that is otherwise reserved for Formula 1 drivers: while a ride on Red Force is far safer than sitting in a real racing car, the experience is no less intense.

Address Avinguda de l'Alcalde Pere Molas, 43480 Vila-seca, Province of Tarragona, Spain | **Getting there** 1.5 hours by train from Barcelona | **Hours** Daily in peak season, closed at times in winter; more information at www.portaventuraworld.com | **Tip** Ferrari Land is part of PortAventura World, with a myriad of other attractions and a water park.

107 Keret House

The narrowest house

In times of housing shortages and increasing rents, creativity in architectural design is in greater demand than ever – especially in the large metropolises. Often, developers simply build upwards in order to create more room for apartments in densely populated cities, or develop their constructions on the last available vacant lots between buildings.

Polish architect Jakub Szczęsny has demonstrated that it takes no more than a small niche to build a complete dwelling: he has created an unusual accommodation in a narrow gap between two houses in Warsaw. His Keret House measures 122 centimetres at its widest point, while at the narrowest it is only 72 centimetres. Even a child could stretch out their arms and touch both facing walls without any difficulty.

Only around 14 square metres of living space are spread across two storeys, yet there is everything available that is needed to live in this unusual accommodation: a bed, a kitchen, a bathroom and a work gallery. Most of the furniture was custom-produced to fit the special dimensions of the house. Thanks to a translucent facade, lots of light shines into the narrow living space, ensuring that it doesn't feel too cramped.

Szczęsny wanted to explore the limits of architectural possibilities with this project, but it took many years from the first concept to its realisation. Getting the necessary authorisation was a particular challenge. According to Polish construction law, the building is too small to be classified as a real residential home, so it is now officially registered as an art installation. Since its completion in 2012, it has already served several artists as a temporary home. The first to use it was the Israeli author Etgar Keret, who gave the house its name. It is open to visitors whenever it is unoccupied, enabling them to discover how much space there is, even in the smallest of homes.

Address Żelazna 74, 00−875 Warsaw, Poland | Getting there The Keret House is in
the Warsaw district of Wola, which is around a 20-minute walk from the main station;
alternatively, take the tram (lines 17, 33, 41) to Hala Mirowska, then on foot. | Hours
Information on guided tours and open days is available at: www.kerethouse.com | Tip
A model of the unusual house at a scale of 1:25 is now part of the famous MoMa
collection in New York.

108 Eisriesenwelt

The largest ice cave

The walk from the cable car to the entrance of the cave takes almost 20 minutes. The round opening in the middle of the rugged rocky landscape has an inconspicuous appearance from a distance. When you stand in front of it, you have a clear view of the peaks and valleys of the Austrian Tennen Mountains from an altitude of 1,640 metres. Then the door opens, and you enter the largest ice cave in Europe.

Warm clothing is essential for a visit, as temperatures inside often remain below freezing, even if it is as hot as mid-summer outside. Visitors are immediately blasted with an icy wind at the entrance, as the cave is subject to the chimney effect: higher and lower lying openings create a strong draught – the prerequisite that so much ice could form in the cave in the first place. In the winter months, cold air flows deep into the mountain. When water then gets into the cave as the snow melts in spring, it freezes there due to the low temperatures. In this way, a whole world of ice was able to form inside the cave over the course of the passing centuries.

The whole cave system stretches over more than 42 kilometres. Only the first kilometre is frozen, and is open to visitors on guided tours. There is no electric light, so tours lead visitors through twisting passages and spacious caves armed with pit lamps. In the dim light it's possible to see icicles hanging from the ceiling, bizarre sculptures, and glittering walls of pure ice.

Some of the bizarre figures have sonorous names, such as 'Hymirburg', 'Odinsaal' or 'Friggas Schleier'. Again and again new formations appear as you pass through this frozen world. The 'Ice Palace' is the last stop. A huge frozen lake covers the entire ground, once apparently used by a pair of skaters as a training area. From here, the visitors are led towards the exit – and back to the welcoming warmth of the Austrian mountains.

Address Eishöhlenstraße 30, 5450 Werfen, Austria | **Getting there** Reach Werfen by train from Salzburg in 45 minutes, then take a shuttle bus to the Eisriesenwelt car park, where a cable car takes visitors to the cave. | **Hours** May–Oct daily from 8.30am | **Tip** Alongside warm clothes, you should also be reasonably fit for a tour through the ice cave: during the 70-minute excursion you'll climb more than 130 metres, and take around 1,400 steps.

109__Ebenezer Place
The shortest street

There are some roads in the world where finding the right house number is not an easy task at all, especially on the long boulevards and avenues of the larger cities. Are the numbers on the buildings climbing or descending? Are there only even numbers on one side of the road, or mixed? The use of half numbers and letters for different entrances makes the whole thing even harder. Every city seems to have its own system, and the search for an address can quickly become a frustrating endeavour.

That can't happen to you on Ebenezer Place in the small Scottish town of Wick, however. Instead, it's much more likely that you won't find the street in the first place, as it's very easy to overlook. The reason? This road is just two metres and six centimetres in length. Former basketball star Dirk Nowitzki would stick out at both ends of the road if he were to make himself comfortable on the pavement! Furthermore, there's only one building – and thus also only one address: unsurprisingly, it's number 1. And yet Ebenezer Place really is its own street, and of course features on the Wick town map.

Scottish bureaucracy is to blame for this unique oddity. When the businessman Alexander Sinclair returned to Scotland from the USA in the 1880s, having made a small fortune there, he decided to open a hotel in the port town of Wick. The Mackays Hotel was built on the junction of Union Street and River Street, right beside the Wick river. The city administration, however, insisted that the small square on the narrow side of the hotel, where the two roads met, also had to have its own road sign. Thus, the address 1 Ebenezer Place was created.

Many may question whether the two metres of asphalt really represent an individual road, but in 2006 its status was confirmed with an entry in the *Guinness Book of Records*. Since then, Ebenezer Place has officially been the shortest street in the world.

Address Ebenezer Place, Wick KW1 5EA, Scotland | **Getting there** Wick is in the far north-east of Scotland. You can reach the town by train from Inverness in almost 4.5 hours. It's a short walk from the station to Ebenezer Place. Alternatively you can also fly to Wick. | **Tip** Wick is surrounded by the Scottish Highlands, which are definitely worth the journey with their green hills and lots of castles and ruins.

110 __ Morske Orgulje
The only sea organ

At first you might believe it's just a couple of steps that lead down to the sea, along the coastal promenade of Zadar. But as you get closer, you can hear it: an idiosyncratic sound beneath the babble of the tourists and the lapping of the waves on the shore. Mysterious tones, at one moment reminiscent of distant church bells, sounding like fog horns or whale songs the next. This is the unique tone of the sea organ, which can only be heard here on the Dalmatian coast.

The Morske Orgulje is surely the most unusual musical instrument anywhere in Europe. This is because it is played by nature. Its inventor is the Croatian architect Nikola Bašić. He had the idea for the project when the harbour promenade of Zadar was being redesigned after the turn of the millennium. He wanted to create a place, in this long-neglected area of the city, where locals and tourists alike would like to spend time and relax – a place to encounter nature.

Bašić presented his unusual instrument to the public in 2005: a sea organ, some 70 metres wide, and laid out over several rows of stone steps. Small, circular openings are set into the steps at regular intervals. Underneath them are positioned 35 tubes of different lengths and widths, each of which has a pipe attached to the end. Through the natural and constantly varying movement of the waves, air is forced into the tubes, and it is this that creates the tones, as in a standard organ. Cavities in the stone stairs serve as resonance chambers amplifying the sound.

The architect's idea captured the public's imagination, and his sea organ has since become the new landmark of the Croatian city. Many people sit here for hours on end to listen to the meditative sounds of the unusual water music. It is especially popular at sunset. After all, Alfred Hitchcock is even said to have called it the most beautiful in the world while on a visit to Zadar.

Address Obala kralja Petra Krešimira IV, 23000 Zadar, Croatia | **Getting there** Reach Zadar by air, bus or boat. The sea organ is at the end of the promenade on a promontory; reach it on foot or by bus (lines 2 and 4). | **Tip** Nikola Bašić also installed the sculpture *Greetings to the Sun* a few steps away from the sea organ. 300 glass plates with integrated solar cells store the sunlight. In the evening they transform into a colourful luminous area, that changes colour in time with the sound of the sea organ.

111___Haus Hiltl
The oldest vegetarian restaurant

Healthy, sustainable, and both climate- and animal-friendly: being vegetarian or vegan is very much on trend these days – and with good reason. What was often considered a fad around 20 years ago has long since become mainstream. Meat-less food is hip and stylish – and an expression of attitude and lifestyle choice.

When the first vegetarian restaurant in Europe, the Vegetarier-heim und Abstinenz Café, opened in Zurich in 1898, things were very different. The Sunday roast was then seen as the epitome of prosperity and a good diet, and vegetarians were often mocked as 'grazers'. The Vegetarierheim was soon given an unflattering nickname too: it was called the 'root bunker' in common parlance. Many of the guests only dared enter the restaurant by the back door, such was their fear of ridicule. Business went extremely badly as a result, and after a few years the restaurant was close to failing.

That the restaurant survived is thanks to the efforts of Ambrosius Hiltl. This tailor's apprentice could no longer practise his career due to suffering from rheumatism. To tackle this, his doctor prescribed strict abstinence from meat, and this is how Hiltl came upon the Vegetarierheim. He took over the struggling business, and made it successful under his own name, together with his future wife, the chef Martha Gneupel. While at first the establishment offered mainly soups and salads, over the following years the menu became increasingly diverse.

Today, Haus Hiltl is a permanent fixture in the Swiss city, and already in the hands of the fourth generation of Hiltls. The small family business has become a veritable empire, with several branches in Zurich, and its own cooking academy. The restaurant even serves typical Swiss dishes such as 'Zürcher Geschnetzeltes' or 'Cordon Bleu' – of course, these are purely vegetarian, made with seitan or tofu.

Address Sihlstraße 28, 8001 Zurich, Switzerland | **Getting there** The restaurant is in Zurich city centre, around 10 minutes' walk from the main station. The nearest tram stop is Rennweg (lines 6, 7, 10, 11 and 13). | **Hours** Mon–Sat 6am–11pm, Sun 8am–11pm | **Tip** In 2013, the Hiltl family opened the first vegetarian butcher's shop in Switzerland, right next to the restaurant. Here you can buy a number of products, ranging from steak tartare and sausage to Sunday roasts, all made with meat substitutes.

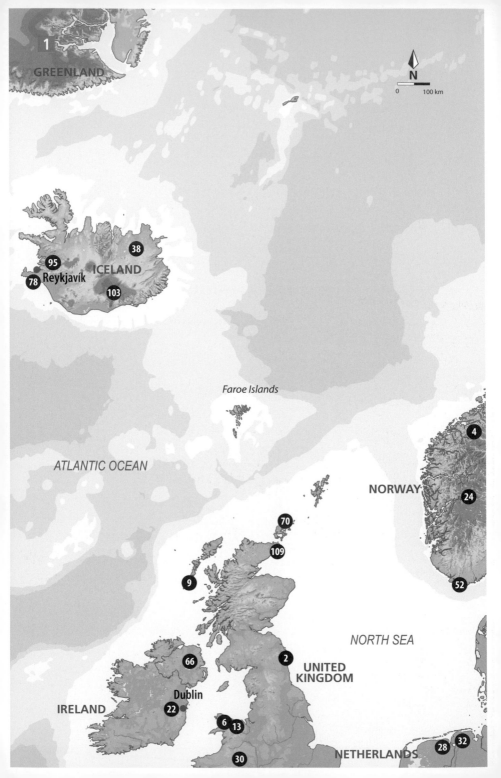

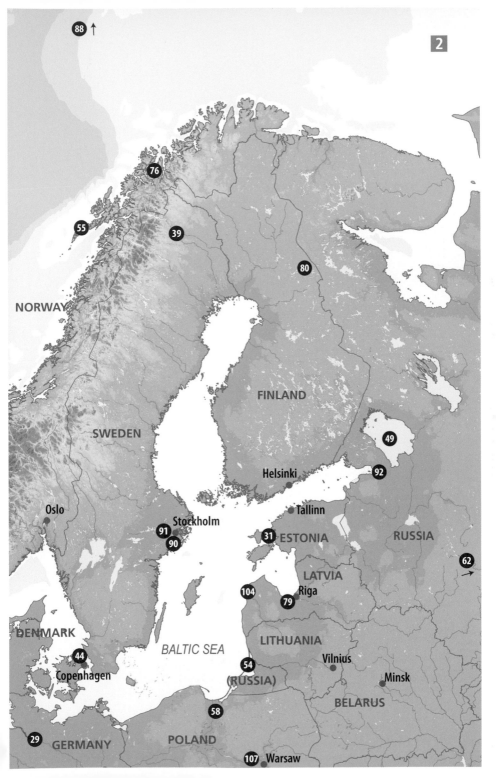

2

NORWAY

SWEDEN

FINLAND

Helsinki

Stockholm

Oslo

ESTONIA

Tallinn

RUSSIA

LATVIA

Riga

BALTIC SEA

DENMARK

Copenhagen

LITHUANIA

Vilnius

(RUSSIA)

BELARUS

Minsk

GERMANY

POLAND

Warsaw

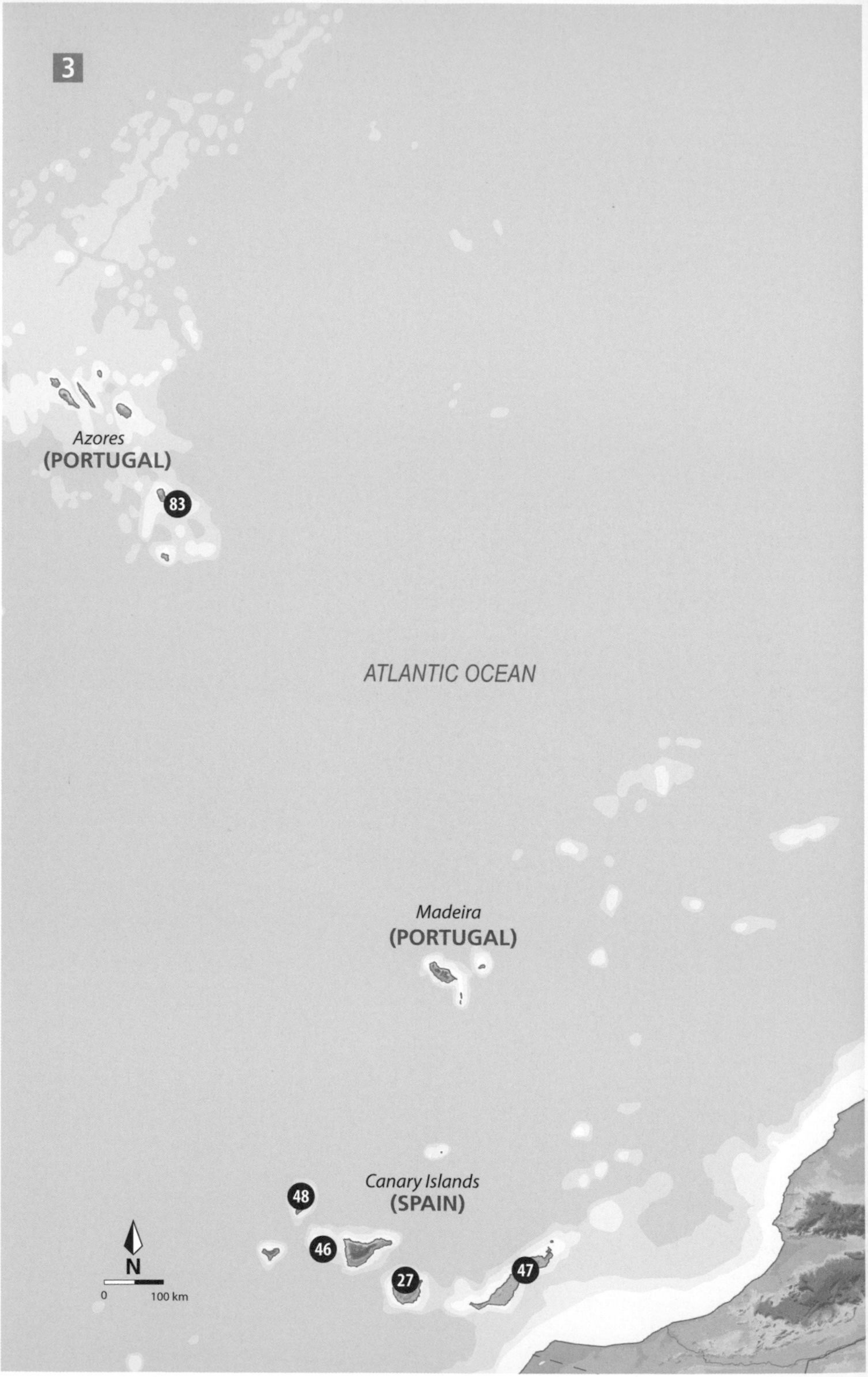

3

Azores
(PORTUGAL)

83

ATLANTIC OCEAN

Madeira
(PORTUGAL)

Canary Islands
(SPAIN)

48

46

27

47

N

0   100 km

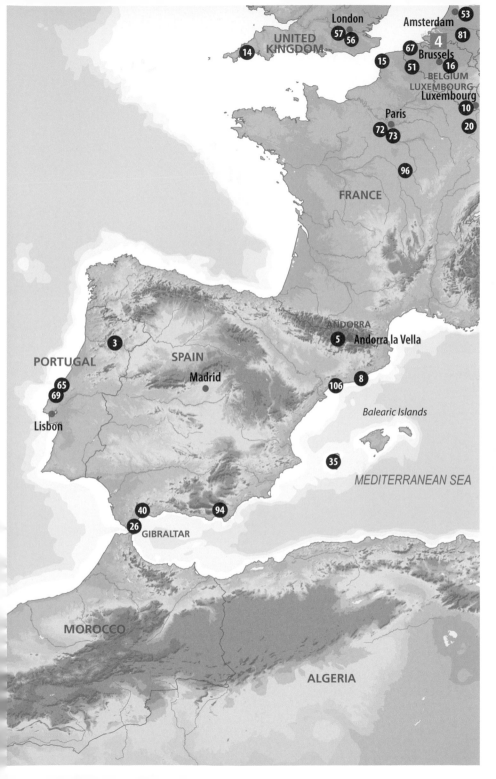

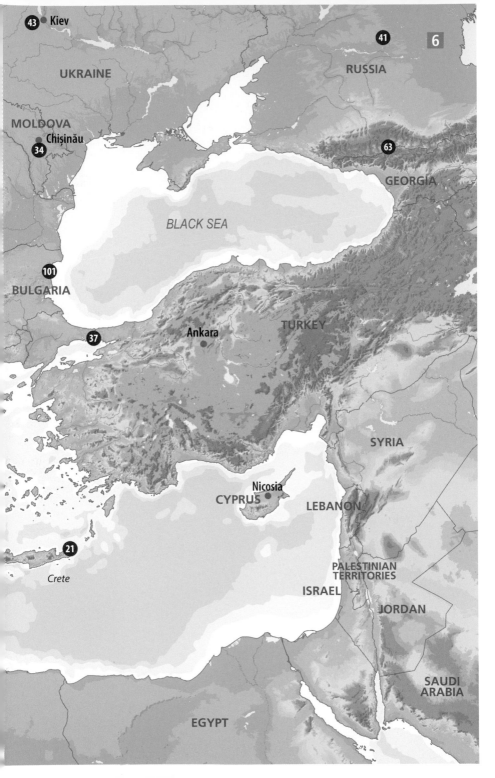

Photographs

Chapter 1, Fonderia Marinelli: shutterstock.com/SerFeo
Chapter 2, Alnwick Poison Garden, top: WikimediaCommons/CC/Amanda Slater,
  bottom: pixabay.com/Rhiannon
Chapter 3, Alto Douro: shutterstock.com/Gi Cristovao Photography
Chapter 4, Trollveggen: Wikimedia Commons/CC/Ximonic (Simo Räsänen)
Chapter 5, Andorra la Vella: shutterstock/Anibal Trejo
Chapter 6, Llanfairpwllgwyngyllgogerychwyrndrobwllllantysiliogogogoch, top:
  shutterstock.com/HildaWeges Photography, bottom: Wikimedia Commons/gemeinfrei
Chapter 7, Fuggerei, top and bottom: pixabay.com/bboellinger
Chapter 8, Camp Nou: shutterstock.com/Iakov Filimonov
Chapter 9, Barra Airport: Gönna Ketels, Deutsche Welle
Chapter 10, Aire de Berchem, top and bottom: Kris Van de Sande
Chapter 11, Zoological Garden: shutterstock.com/hanohiki
Chapter 12, Jungfraujoch: pixabay.com/a_v_a
Chapter 13, Velocity 2: mauritius images/Nigel Wilkins/Alamy
Chapter 14, Eden Project: shutterstock.com/Anna Jastrzebska
Chapter 15, Nausicaá: pixabay.com/VIVIANE6276
Chapter 16, Delirium Café: shutterstock.com/EWY Media
Chapter 17, Palace of the Parliament: shutterstock.com/Tupungato
Chapter 18, Budapest: shutterstock.com/LongJon
Chapter 19, Athos: shutterstock.com/Dimitris Panas
Chapter 20, Mondial Air Ballons: shutterstock.com/OSTILL is FRanck Camhi
Chapter 21, Vai Beach: shutterstock.com/Georgios Tsichlis
Chapter 22, Christ Church Cathedral: shutterstock.com/Quintanilla
Chapter 23, Tara River Canyon: shutterstock.com/Martin Lehmann
Chapter 24, Ice Music Festival: mauritius images/Paul Swinney/Alamy
Chapter 25, Labirinto della Masone: shutterstock.com/Amy CChapteri
Chapter 26, Upper Rock Nature Reserve: shutterstock.com/Ben Gingell
Chapter 27, Valle de Agaete: mauritius images/Westend61/Maria Breuer
Chapter 28, Excalibur: shutterstock.com/Annari
Chapter 29, Miniatur Wunderland, top and bottom: Miniatur Wunderland Hamburg
Chapter 30, Hay-on-Wye: shutterstock.com/abcbritain
Chapter 31, Heltermaa-Rohuküla, top and bottom: shutterstock.com/bbbb
Chapter 32, Suurhusen Church Tower: mauritius images/Hartmut Schmidt/imageBROKER
Chapter 33, Hum: shutterstock.com/RudolfsM
Chapter 34, Mileştii Mici: © Mileştii Mici
Chapter 35, Sublimotion, top and bottom: © Sublimotion
Chapter 36, Steinkaulenberg: shutterstock.com/travelview
Chapter 37, Kapalı Çarşı: mauritius images/Axiom RF/Kav Dadfar
Chapter 38, Dettifoss: shutterstock.com/Petr Simon
Chapter 39, Icehotel: shutterstock.com/Viktorishy
Chapter 40, Júzcar: mauritius images/Sebastian Wasek/Alamy
Chapter 41, Kalmykia: Hendrik Welling, Deutsche Welle
Chapter 42, Pyramidenkogel: mauritius images/Udo Siebig
Chapter 43, Arsenalna: shutterstock.com/meunierd
Chapter 44, Dyrehavsbakken: shutterstock.com/Stig Alenas
Chapter 45, Kopaonik Ski Resort: shutterstock.com/Fotosr52
Chapter 46, La Gomera: shutterstock.com/Martina I. Meyer
Chapter 47, Museo Atlántico: shutterstock.com/Sybille Reuter, © VG Bild-Kunst, Bonn 2021
Chapter 48, Roque de los Muchachos Observatory: shutterstock.com/Martin Leber
Chapter 49, Lake Ladoga: shutterstock.com/javarman
Chapter 50, Liechtenstein: shutterstock.com/stifos
Chapter 51, Braderie de Lille: shutterstock.com/MisterStock
Chapter 52, Under: shutterstock.com/Lillian Tveit
Chapter 53, Keukenhof: shutterstock.com/Kit Leong
Chapter 54, The Curonian Spit: shutterstock.com/Majonit
Chapter 55, Unstad: shutterstock.com/czechexplorerphotography
Chapter 56, British Library: shutterstock.com/cowardlion

© Mark Hayes

Patricia Szilagyi is a freelance journalist and author living in Berlin. For more than 10 years, she has been working as an editor for the magazine 'Euromaxx' in the Deutsche Welle programme. There, she works intensively with the diverse cultures and lifestyles in Europe. Travelling is her great passion – she sets out as often as possible to discover Europe and the world – not always chasing records, but constantly looking for new places and inspiration.